ENDORSE

MW00651189

In his first book, *Becoming Your Own Banker*, Nelson Nash completely annihilates the pecuniary mythos which classifies whole life insurance as being "too costly." He accomplishes this by diligently illustrating how participating whole life insurance, when designed and used for its "living benefits," becomes the most valuable financial tool which you can still personally control.

With *Building Your Warehouse of Wealth,* Nelson takes off the gloves by challenging you to revolutionize and transform the way you THINK! Because the way you think creates the building blocks for your own "Warehouse of Wealth."

—Dr. Tomas P. McFie

Stephen R. Covey, best-selling author and recognized as one of *Time* magazine's 25 most influential Americans often quips that for every 100 people hacking away at the braches of a problem, there is one "chopping at the roots". When it comes to understanding the financial challenges and opportunities facing us today and that neither Washington nor Wall Street can provide the answer, Nelson Nash is that man chopping at the root of the problem.

While the financial entertainers and self-appointed gurus are looking for Government and investment solutions to improve our financial well being Nelson has gone to the heart of the problem. Nash points out that our access to capital and our ability to create and control our own markets through the ancient process of banking predates all Federal programs and solutions and is far more reliable and efficient.

Quit wasting your time trying to find the hot investment of the day or the next hot tax strategy as your ticket to financial nirvana. Read everything you can get your hands on by R. Nelson Nash then IMPLEMENT these simple yet profoundly important concepts!

You owe it to yourself and your family to create and control your 'Warehouse of Wealth'; the consequences of NOT having your own Warehouse are life changing.

—Jim Kindred, Financial
Strategies Group, LLC

In *Building Your Warehouse of Wealth*, Nelson Nash provides another generous helping of his inimitable wit and financial wisdom. Longtime fans will recognize the themes, but will be delighted by new material and insights. This book may be the single best introduction to Nash's worldview, which focuses on the benefits of whole life insurance but is infused with Nelson's faith in God and distrust in politicians!

—Robert P. Murphy, Ph.D.

There is, to my knowledge, no one more passionate about economic freedom and the personal liberty it engenders than Nelson Nash. His prescription for human happiness is simple: follow the teachings of Christ and learn how to remove oneself from the bondage imposed by governments, banks, and Wall Street.

Having followed Nelson's ideas and having implemented them with hundreds of clients, I can honestly say that they are fresh, vibrant, full of good common sense, and accessible to anyone.

Building Your Warehouse of Wealth takes Nelson's original concept of "infinite banking" and amplifies it, addressing on a deeper level many of the most frequently asked questions about how to properly construct these plans to achieve maximum benefits.

Building Your Warehouse of Wealth is, of course, imbued with Nelson's philosophy that personal freedom and responsibility are impossible to achieve without access to, and control of, one's wealth. The "end run" around conventional money wisdom foisted upon us by financial pundits, Wall Street, and banks, says Nelson, is to create life insurance-based plans that offer flexibility, liquidity, and control of personal wealth.

Reading this book will give you unparalleled insights into the real truth about money, why it makes sense to control your own financial future, and a plan for making it happen. I highly recommend it to anyone who wants to chart a new course for their financial future.

—TERESA KUHN JD RFC CSA

This is a written testament of who you are, Nelson. Reading this was like having you sitting across from me in my living room. In the years I have known you, I have heard you talk about all of this in one form or another. This is because it is not just in your head; it's in your heart. It spells out in clear language the problem and the solution. Everyone will be immensely blessed to read this book.

—CARLOS LARA, NASHVILLE,
TN CO-AUTHOR OF *HOW
PRIVATIZED BANKING REALLY WORKS*

I am a blessed individual for so many reasons, but the LORD has increased my blessings by knowing Nelson Nash. His book "Becoming Your Own Banker," came into my life in 2002, and I have not been the same. I was the conventional Financial Planner at that time with all the initials after my name to prove it, but it was all a lie.

I found the truth in BYOB, and have taken every opportunity to spend time with and to listen to Nelson for over ten (10) years. Now, having read Nelson's latest book "Building Your Warehouse of Wealth," it is like having him with me whenever I want. As I read it, the thought that was running through my soul was, what will I do with this information.

I, my family, and agents at Alpha & Omega Financial Services will continue to teach this truth, with documentation to those individuals who have a teachable spirit, who want to learn the truth about money, how it works, and how they can break the bonds of financial slavery that the world wants to put them in. As Nelson says on p. 15 of BYOB, "This is going to take some time and expense," but oh, is it worth it! Thank you, Nelson for standing for the truth.

—RAY POTEET,
ALPHA & OMEGA FINANCIAL SERVICES

In 2005, after 14 years of success in the life insurance and financial services industry, several designations and literally thousands of hours or training and CE coursework, I finally learned the truth about money because of the inspired, original work of R. Nelson Nash in *Becoming Your Own Banker*.

It is an absolutely powerful, yet simple paradigm shift in the economic thinking and human action of the individual.

Now with *Building Your Warehouse of Wealth,* Nelson eloquently expands the understanding of money, human action and the power of the reader's thinking. Nelson's mentor, Leonard E. Read, would be proud.

Building Your Warehouse of Wealth and *Becoming Your Own Banker* should be required reading of every life insurance agent, insurance company home office employee and every financial practitioner of any sort.

As a matter of fact, this is an absolute must read if you have any interest in the truth about money.

—JAMES C. NEATHERY, 20+ YEAR VETERAN OF THE LIFE
INSURANCE AND FINANCIAL SERVICES INDUSTRY.

"Building Your Warehouse of Wealth is an excellent adventure exploring God's plan for taking dominion in this world. Anyone interested in throwing off the shackles of this world will find in it many useful insights about building and holding wealth in a lost world. Moreover, because the author has thought deeply about the history of Israel, the reader will also gain new insights into the Scriptures. I highly recommend it to you."

—PAUL A. CLEVELAND, PH.D.
PROFESSOR OF ECONOMICS AND FINANCE
BIRMINGHAM SOUTHERN COLLEGE

Building Your

Warehouse of Wealth

A Grassroots Method of Avoiding
Fractional Reserve Banking—*Think About it!*

R. Nelson Nash

Infinite Banking Concept™, LLC

Birmingham, Alabama

© Copyright 2012 R. Nelson Nash

Infinite Banking Concept™, LLC
2957 Old Rocky Ridge Road
Birmingham, AL 35243

Email: david@infinitebanking.org
www.infinitebanking.org
205-276-2977

ISBN 978-0-9726316-5-5 (Paperback)
ISBN 978-0-9726316-6-2 (ePUB)
ISBN 978-0-9726316-7-9 (Kindle/Mobi)
ISBN 978-0-9726316-8-6 (ePDF)

Published by Infinite Banking Concept™, LLC

No part of this publication may be reproduced, stored in a retrieval
system, or transmitted in any form by any means, electronic,
mechanical, photocopy, recording, or otherwise without prior
written permission of Nelson Nash, except for brief quotations in
publications.

Cover illustration: iStockphoto © Leontura,
Cover illustration modification by RD Studio
Book design by DesignForBooks.com

ACKNOWLEDGEMENTS

There are those who have been extremely helpful to me in producing this book. First of all, I thank David Stearns for his expertise in all the administrative work that is necessary along with editing suggestions and proofreading.

Also, to Dr. Barry Nash, Dr. Tom McFie, Robert P. Murphy, PhD, Paul Cleveland, PhD, Raymond Poteet, Jim Kindred, Dan Rust, Larry Byrd, James Neathery, Teresa Kuhn, Carlos Lara, and Tim Yurek for their help in reading the manuscript and making helpful comments and suggestions.

And, a very special thanks to Todd Langford for the section of the book that he provided on the subject of Equity Indexed Universal Life, a topic that I felt incompetent to address.

To all of you, I am humbled by your willingness to help in this endeavor.

This book is dedicated to
all those who are practicing
The Infinite Banking Concept
in their everyday lives.

CONTENTS

INTRODUCTION

*Action is preceded by thinking. Thinking is to
deliberate beforehand over future action and to reflect
afterwards upon the past action. Thinking and action
are inseparable.*

—LUDWIG VON MISES

*Thoughts lead on to purposes; purposes go forth in
action; actions form habits; habits decide character;
and character fixes our destiny.*

—TRYON EDWARDS

I finished college in 1952 at the University of Georgia with a BS Degree in Forestry. While there I took the four years of Air Force ROTC and this financial help made it possible for me to graduate. A two year obligation of active duty was required and this was right in the middle of the Korean Conflict. Our government called it "a police action" instead of a war, because only Congress can declare war on another country. Somehow or another, government leaders try to change the meaning of words and still accomplish their objectives—but, in this case it still was a war. Nevertheless, 54,246 American men and women lost their lives in the event.

Casualties are not included in this figure. But, to me, the worst result of that war was the **thought process** that it produced in the minds of American citizens. There is no way that this activity could be classified as "defending our freedoms." *How you think is everything.* It determines your behavior.

Upon completion of this obligation I went to work as a forester in Eastern North Carolina. I knew very little about Socialism and its effect on the minds of people, but I came face-to-face with the mental paralysis that this monster causes. Consider this situation: Johnston County, NC is tobacco country. It was a much bigger factor in the economy at that time than now. Twenty acres was a typical tobacco farm. So, here I am working in that kind of situation.

I call on (we will call him Mr. Smith) and he owned 5,000 acres of land. Four thousand acres were in timberland, and 1,000 acres were farmland. He had accumulated all this property to qualify for the 100 acres of tobacco allotment that went with the farmland. You see, tobacco production was a highly regulated by the Department of Agriculture—bureaucracy at its best!

"Mr. Smith, I am a private forester—I do not work for the government in any capacity (Smoky Bear and I don't see things exactly the same.) I work for people like you by contract. With your agreement I will inventory your timberland for a fee and will bring you a report of my findings. I will divide your timberland up into three categories; good, bad, and indifferent. I will propose that you sell the bad and indifferent timber and use the proceeds to rejuvenate the forest land with good trees. Make this procedure an on-going practice and you will have a constant source of income in the future."

His response, "I can't do that." My reply, "Would you mind telling me why not?" "I know the government pays landowners to grow trees. Whatever they will pay for, I will agree to do." Now, look, by the time you consider the value of what little the government would allocate, plus the time and effort of the landowner abiding by the bureaucratic procedures, etc., any landowner has spent more than the value received—not to mention the time value of all the loss of production on the land containing "bad and marginal" timber.

I ran into that kind of thinking in the majority of cases of calling on timberland owners that had substantial acreage. So, I wondered, "Why would anyone behave like that? Why don't people do what common sense indicates would be best to do?" After experiencing this phenomenon many times, here I am at a social gathering at the home of a Radiologist and I'm "running my mouth" about what I had witnessed.

The Radiologist says, "Sounds like you need to read this book." He went back to his library and got a copy of Economics In One Lesson by Henry Hazlitt. "Try reading this."

About ten days later I returned the book and said, "I have two questions—Where have you folks been hiding this stuff—and why did you hide it from me?" He replied, "If you liked what you read, get on the mailing list for this journal called The Freeman, published by The Foundation for Economic Education. All you have to do is ask for it. They are supported entirely by donations—but they will never ask you for money. It is all dependent on your evaluation of what you are reading. If you have not sent them a contribution within one year, they will simply take your name off the mailing list."

Well, needless to say, I got on the list immediately and the more I read, the better it got. That began my passionate study of Austrian Economics. I was particularly attracted to the writings of Leonard E. Read and the Historian, Dr. Clarence B. Carson. In time to come, Leonard became my mentor and friend. I am a Charter Member of the Leonard E. Read Society. There are only one hundred of us. Later on I got to know Dr. Clarence Carson very well. My wife and I worked with him on his Board of Directors for over 20 years.

One day I was reading The Freeman and I read an excellent article by Dr. Paul Cleveland, an Economics Professor at Birmingham Southern College, located right here in my city. Within hours I was talking with him and within days we were having lunch together. Soon afterward I introduced him to Dr. Carson and later he became involved as a member of Carson's Board of Directors. During their friendship Clarence taught Paul how to write books and self-publish them. Paul has written several since and they are listed in the reading list in the back of this book.

By the grace of God, I was there in Irvington-on-Hudson, NY when Leonard E. Read died, and when Dr. Clarence B. Carson died, Paul Cleveland and I were asked to conduct the funeral. As the Psalmist David says in Psalm 23:5, "My cup runneth over!"

And so, after many years of study of Austrian Economics I discover the answer to my question about the behavior of Mr. Smith, the timberland owner in Eastern North Carolina and all the others with similar behavior. Why didn't these timber landowners just forget about the government programs and do what common sense tells them to do? They would have been much better off. It is simply the fact that, whenever there is a government program of any kind, normally intelligent people will abandon their productive activity, and go stand in line for their share of the measly handout—and watch each other starve to death! It all depends on how one *thinks!* Socialism does this sort of thing to the minds of men. It is all a form of covetousness. *Thou shalt not covet* is the last of the Ten

Commandments. In order to become a free man, one cannot do that—it will dominate his thinking and that will determine his actions.

In early 1957 I was attending the regular meeting of the Lions Club in Smithfield, NC. The program chairman played the LP recording of Earl Nightingale's message, The Strangest Secret. What an impact it had on my life! I could not wait to get my personal copy of that record.

> *The Strangest Secret—You become what you think about all day long.*
>
> —EARL NIGHTINGALE

> *For as he thinks in his heart, so is he.*
>
> —PROVERBS 23:7

> *As A Man Thinketh*
>
> —JAMES ALLEN

I listened to that message so many times that I memorized it. It is true! You *do* become what you *think about.* While I was in the second through fourth grade, growing up in Athens, GA, we lived across the road from the airport. I'm just a kid, watching those airplanes regularly and *thinking* about what it would be like to be a pilot. I *knew* that, one day, I would become a pilot though I had no earthly idea of how it would come to pass. Just six years later, I made my first solo flight at that airport!

Being involved with airplanes is expensive stuff—and my family was not noted for having lots of money. But, if you have the desire, somehow or another, it *will* take place. Be careful of what you think about—it is going to happen! Earl

Nightingale says, "The mind is like a field. The field doesn't care what you plant there, it will grow. Plant good thoughts and you will become good. Plant bad thoughts and you will become bad. Plant nothing and you will become nothing!"

1957 was a good year in my life. That was the year that I started my own business, in addition to the items mentioned above. I became involved with the local Chamber of Commerce. Later that year the Chamber sponsored the Dale Carnegie Course and I enrolled. I remember vividly in one of the books we studied how the notorious gangster, Al Capone, *thought* that his activity was a benefit to mankind! That was quite a revelation to me. Didn't he know better? No! That was the way he ***thought*** and thoughts determine behavior.

All the events listed in this introduction led me to many years of study of human behavior and why people behave the way they do. A vital item in their behavior revolves around how they look at money and wealth. Conventional wisdom has led the world into financial slavery. It doesn't have to be that way. There is a way out of this bondage. My prayer is that you will find this book helpful in finding your own way to financial freedom. Any necessary change in your life will involve the way you **think** and your willingness to change the way you go about it.

BUILDING YOUR

Warehouse
of Wealth

A Grassroots Method of Avoiding
Fractional Reserve Banking—*Think About it!*

1

STORING WEALTH

Five percent of the people think. Ten percent think
that they think; and the other eighty-five percent
would rather die than think.

—THOMAS ALVA EDISON

Many people believe they are thinking when,
actually, they are only rearranging their prejudices.

—LEONARD E. READ

Throughout history mankind has developed means of improving his standard of living. He built and accumulated wealth and needed a storehouse of his efforts and ideas. Personal property—wealth has taken on many forms. Job 1:2 in the Bible tells us Job had seven sons and three daughters, and he owned seven thousand sheep, three thousand camels, five hundred yoke of oxen and five hundred donkeys, and had a large number of servants. He was the greatest man among all the people of the East.

Seven thousand sheep is a lot of sheep! I can visualize that this was a valuable source of wool for garments and food for their own sustenance. Three thousand camels surely had to do with transportation of goods. Somehow, I can't conceive of camels being a source of food for his people! Five hundred yoke of oxen indicates that there were one thousand individual oxen and I can imagine they were used for tilling the land to grow crops. And there were five hundred donkeys, again, beasts of burden to solve the matter of transportation for people and goods for trade.

All those animals required a lot of care and food for their own sustenance. How did he keep up with all this stuff? Maybe he had an abacus, but he didn't have a way to make a record of his calculations. Can you imagine life without a computer plus a printer/fax/scanner machine?

It also took a large manpower pool to look after all those animals, too. It was no wonder that he had "a large number of servants." His overhead cost had to be very high. What if he lived in the U.S.A. today and had to factor in all those "fringe benefits" to them! But, my point of concern is, *where did he keep all this wealth?* No evidence is presented that he stole all these animals. But, how did he keep *others* from stealing his? Surely, he had to have some place to *store this wealth.*

Genesis 13:2 tells us Abram (before his name was changed to Abraham) had become very wealthy in livestock and in silver and gold. Here we see the wealth in the form of livestock again, but now he has additional wealth in the form of gold and silver. These precious metals concentrated wealth and made it much more compact and manageable. It was easily divisible, limited in quantity and was accepted by others as a store of value, thus making trade much more efficient than barter to get the things of life that we need or want.

But, those metals are *heavy!* Specially, if you have a lot of them! You don't want to have to lug that stuff all around. I don't even carry around our relatively worthless coins in my pockets today. Try making that a habit over a long period of time and you could easily wear a hole in your pockets!

So, this presents a problem—where do you *store* all this gold and silver? Well, what about seeing a person who deals with gold and silver—goldsmiths and silversmiths? They could warehouse the metals and provide guards for round-the-clock security against theft. The smiths could give the owners of the gold and silver deposits receipts for the amount of the metals left in their care. The smiths earned a fee for their efforts—and when the owners needed some gold of silver they went to the warehouse, surrendered some receipts and got the metal to conduct their business. Of course, the owners had to pay the smiths for their services.

Consider what Forrest McDonald reports in his book, *Novus Ordo Seclorum*, page 115: "One was the tobacco warehouse system, as regularized by a Virginia Act of 1748, which became the prototype for other acts in other tobacco-growing colonies/states. Under the Virginia statute, planters deposited their tobacco in public warehouses and received in exchange notes that were not only freely negotiable but also **legal tender.**" Tobacco played a significant role in the economy of getting these colonies established.

The receipts could just as well be used in trade and commerce, hence, avoiding the necessity of a trip to the warehouse to get the precious metals and complete business transactions. This became common practice many years ago and left the door wide open to one of mankind's basic problems—the propensity to steal! Face up to it, that was the first labor-saving device—

theft! Don't produce anything yourself, but just steal what others produce! And there are all kinds of sophisticated ways to steal.

> *Give a man a gun and he can rob a bank. Give a man a bank and he can rob the world.*
>
> —JIM TROTTER

> *Banking establishments are more dangerous than standing armies.*
>
> —THOMAS JEFFERSON

The precious metal warehouse owners noticed that all that stuff that belonged to others was "just sitting there" and earning nothing. "Our customers are not *all* going to reclaim their gold and silver at the same time. These people have become accustomed to accepting these receipts as negotiable instruments. Why don't we just print up lots of receipts? We can lend those receipts and earn interest on them. The customers will never notice the difference." And, so, the world got introduced into the "fractional reserve lending system." This led to the use of paper money throughout the world. Today, your local commercial bank can lend ten dollars for every dollar that depositors have left with them. For a complete explanation of this process I suggest you read *How Privatized Banking Really Works* by Carlos Lara & Robert P. Murphy, PhD. Also, read *The Mystery of Banking* by Murray N. Rothbard. There are lots of additional books available on the market, but these two are a good place to start. Study them and get informed on what is *really* happening to your money! You need to know.

Banks lend money that doesn't exist! That is *fraud*! If any other business did that, they would be *thrown under the jail*. But, this has gone on so long that the practice has become *normal*. People accept it and think nothing of it! They let bankers do their *thinking* for them! Preposterous!

> *It is well enough that people of the nation do not understand our banking and monetary system, for if they did, I believe there would be a revolution before tomorrow morning.*
>
> —Henry Ford

To make matters worse, we now come to recognize *the ultimate confidence game*—a central bank—in the U.S. it is called The Federal Reserve System. The "Banker's Bank." The lender of last resort. For a great explanation of this matter, please read *The Creature From Jekyll Island* by G. Edward Griffin. This book is a *must read*. Griffin explains that The Federal Reserve Bank is not Federal, it is not a bank, and there is no reserve—it is a *cartel* among bankers.

The Austrian school of economic thought has the best explanation of the business cycle. Central Banks inflate the money supply with fiat money (worthless paper), people think they have something and spend this money recklessly, and reality eventually sets in—and it always comes crashing down. It happens over a long period of time and people don't see it happening to them. But, remember, the *primary* source of inflation in the U.S. is your local commercial bank. The Fed is there to bail out the banks in case they get into trouble with their lending practices.

This brings us to our problem today, **where are you going to warehouse your wealth**—your money? Banks make money by lending money that doesn't exist. Isn't it pretty obvious that, if no one made a loan at a bank, they would have no customers and would have to change their business? Therefore, if you have a loan at a regular commercial bank, ***then you are part of the problem!*** Think about it!

> *On the American money market today it is no*
> *longer the banks, it is the insurance companies that*
> *are the greatest money lenders. And the money*
> *of the insurance company is—not legally, but*
> *economically—the property of the insured. And*
> *practically everybody in the United States is insured*
> *in one way or another.*
>
> —FROM *HUMAN ACTION* BY LUDWIG VON MISES

Fortunately, there is a place where wealth can be accumulated and stored that does not engage in lending money that does not exist. It has been around for over 200 years and is widely accepted. There are millions of people who participate in the practice. It is Dividend-paying Whole Life Insurance with a Mutual Company—one that is owned by its policy holders. There are no stockholders.

Life Insurance policy owners pay premiums to a Mutual Life Insurance Company. (They buy Life Insurance) This forms a large pool of money because there are lots of people participating in the idea. This pool of money is now the property of the life insurance *company—it is not the property of the policy owners. (*Go back and read the quotation by Ludwig von Mises as many times as necessary until you completely understand his thought). To be able to pay the guaranteed death benefit the company has agreed to pay, the company must put this pool of money to work by making investments, loaning money, joint ventures, etc. Look at the financial statement of any substantial mutual life insurance company and you will see that most of the investments are very conserva-

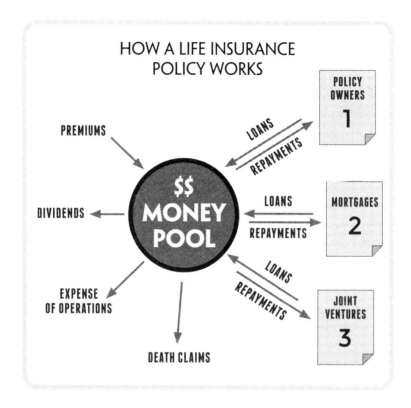

Figure 1. How a Participating Whole Life Insurance Policy works

tive things, like bonds—things that have a **guaranteed repayment schedule.**

They are not looking for a "high rate of return." They are concerned with stability in the financial world. (Caveat: This is not true of products called Universal Life, Variable Life, Equity Indexed Universal Life, etc.)

In Figure 1 you will note there are three places that they can—and do—make investments. I wanted to establish a hierarchy of **certain places** they put money to work. Money goes out and money comes back in. Notice that the Joint

Ventures, shopping centers, real estate, etc. ranks number 3. At the major intersection of the down-town Birmingham, AL financial district there are three high-rise buildings— all financed or owned by one major life insurance company. South of the city, there is a huge real estate development. It is about forty years old at this time. It was a joint venture by the same life insurance company and a major construction company.

Later on there was a very large shopping mall and hotel built in this same area. It was all financed by another major life insurance company. But, all of this type of activity bears a certain amount of risk. In the Eastern part of our city, there is another large shopping mall that opened in 1975. There were four "anchor stores" plus more than 100 other stores. By 2009 the entire mall was totally vacant. To avoid as much of this type of risk as possible, investment officials at these insurance companies are pretty well paid for their expertise. I don't know who financed this project initially but the vacant property is now owned by the Howard Hughes Corporation. Whatever the case, this mall was operating for 34 years and the company that financed it probably recovered all the money they risked plus the interest they earned during the amortization period.

I have seen certain "strip malls" and other such ventures that did not last that long. You can find such examples all over the country.

Investments that have lesser risk are business and residential mortgages. This type of activity ranks #2 in the diagram. These are "conventional mortgages"—20% down—conservative loans. Not "sub-prime" stuff. Every month the borrower makes a payment, the strength of the lender increases. The borrower owes less and less and the lender has a mortgage on the entire amount. This activity doesn't require the high cost home-office expertise.

So, with the high cost of overhead and the high risk involved with #3 in the diagram, and the lower cost overhead and lower risk in #2—I don't see a great deal of difference in the results back to the company. Why do they bother with the #3 stuff? Frankly, there is the possibility of a higher yield—otherwise they wouldn't do it.

Now, please turn your attention to #1 in the diagram—the policy owners. The insurance company will lend money to them—up to the amount of **equity** each person has in the policy (the cash value at any particular time). That is 100% of whatever can be lent from that owner's policy values! The owner is using the cash value as collateral to obtain a loan from the insurance company, which now holds a lien against any potential death benefit check it has to pay the owner. There is some (though rather small) risk in the other invest-ments the insurance company makes. The loans to policy-holders, however, are **totally secure**. Thus, it is obvious that the owner outranks every other possible borrower in access to money (cash values in his policy) that the insurance com-pany must put to work in order to be able to pay the promised death benefit. What's more, the insurance company cannot lend out money that doesn't exist the way a local commer-cial bank does. Hence, they cannot inflate the money supply!

Since it is true, that a policy owner can borrow up to 100% of whatever can be lent from his policy at any point in time, then this means that the owner has absolute and total control over the lending function of the insurance company as it relates to the equity in his policy. In essence, the policy owner is saying to the company, "I don't have a use for the money right now, so put it to work with your other possible customers." Notice that this means the values in his policy are ***always at work at any one time***. Contrast this with the situation of the gold in the warehouse of the goldsmiths years ago. The gold was "just sitting there, earning nothing."

When a policyholder requests a policy loan, the life insurance company has to actually *get* that money from somewhere, either from incoming premium payments or by selling off other assets. The life insurance company can't simply create the new loan out of thin air. Remember the temptation of the warehouse owners to print up "bogus receipts" thus inflating the money supply. **The Life Insurance Companies cannot inflate.**

What about this idea of making loans? Many people hear the word "loan" and immediately their brain goes into "deep freeze." A loan equals something "bad." It a truism that "you finance everything that you buy—you either borrow from some other source (and pay interest) or you use your own money (and give up the opportunity to earn interest)—there are no exceptions." It is known as the concept of "lost opportunity cost." We learned that principle back in 1949 in Forestry School. The professor told us, "You are going to be teaching clients how to grow trees. That means he is going to spend money *today* to get those seedlings in the ground and he won't get anything back for *25 years*. That money spent was 'borrowed money.'" Our reply, "Oh, no, Professor, that money was from my client's checking account—it had no cost." The professor replied, "Your client *could have been earning interest* somewhere else instead. You must remember 'lost opportunity cost,' otherwise you are deceiving yourself and your client. Fooling either party is not a good idea! Don't ever forget that fact."

It is amazing how "smart businessmen" give lip-service to this concept, yet they don't obey it in their personal and business activities! Years ago when I was active in the Life Insurance business, I was calling on a very prominent Wholesale Drug firm. The owner had his CPA involved in the presentation. I brought up the concept of lost opportunity and the CPA said, "Oh no, our money does not have a cost." I found a way to terminate the interview as gracefully as possible soon afterward. There is no way that you can teach an established fact to a person with such a mindset. That's the way he feels.

> *Feelings are facts to those who have them.*
> —LARRY WILSON, WILSON LEARNING CORP.

In addition, there is the case of Stern-Stewart Consulting Firm in New York. Back in September 1993 there was a cover story in FORTUNE magazine about Stern-Stewart and their development of the concept of Economic Value Added (EVA). The article cited some very prominent firms that were their clients. It seems these "smart businessmen" in these internationally known firms had somehow forgotten (or maybe they never knew) the concept of lost opportunity cost—and so they were paying Stern-Stewart handsome consulting fees to teach them this fundamental fact. Amazing!! **It is all about how one thinks!** When their clients started practicing their teachings the value of the stocks of the companies took off like a rocket, because investors now saw that "this is a company whose values are going to get better every day." (By the way, that is exactly how all my Dividend-paying Whole Life Insurance policies work. The cash values got bigger yesterday, they got bigger today and I *know they will get bigger tomorrow!*)

Why, there is even one financial guru out there who thinks he invented the idea of lost opportunity cost. Maybe he never heard of an Irishman named Richard Cantillon (1680–1734) who was probably the first to isolate the fact. And there was also the essay by Frederic Bastiat (1850) *What Is Seen and What Is Not Seen*. So, the concept has been around for quite some time.

When you take out a loan at a bank, it is an ***asset*** of the bank and is producing income in the form of interest on the loan. When you make a deposit to your bank account, that is a ***liability*** of the bank—they owe you that amount. Hence, if you own your Warehouse of Wealth you want to make **loans** from your warehouse and pay it interest. The higher the interest you pay your system, the more profitable it becomes. When you do so, your system is earning interest that would be going to some other financial institution.

Forty years ago a Senior Vice-President of First National Bank of Birmingham told me, "If the depositors of a bank could read the financial statement of the bank—and understand what it really means—they would never put their money there." Such is the world in which we live.

Let's go back to Figure 1. As a result of what you have seen so far, there is an ever-increasing pool of cash coming into the life insurance company. Every once in a while (it doesn't happen all that often) some policy owner dies. When this happens, the company must pay the beneficiary from its pool of money.

Actuaries are the "engineers" in the concept of life insurance. They are dealing with a pool of ten million selected lives—people who have been through a "screening process." When a person applies for life insurance he must pass a physical exam of some kind to prevent what is known as "adverse selection against the company." And they are dealing with a theoretical life span of 121 years (not long ago it was 100 years, but thanks to increased life spans this projection has been recently increased).

Looking at the next item in the diagram, the company must pay the cost of operating the company. This comes out of the pool of cash, also.

Once a year, the Directors of the company meet to determine the *Dividend Scale* for the coming year that will be equitably distributed to the policy owners. As you will learn in the following section, those dividends can become enormous over a long period of time.

CLASSIFICATION

While I was in Forestry School in the early 50's we had lots of courses that involved **classification**. Dendrology, the study of classification of trees, lasted all year long! Take a number of such courses and maybe it will dawn on you that it is important to classify things on the basis of their **major characteristics**— not incidental ones.

For instance, have you ever cut an apple in half? Cut it through the **equator**—*not* **the poles**—and open it up. You will find a **5-pointed star** pattern in the arrangement of the seeds. That's because the apple is in the **Rose Family**. Every plant in the Rose family has 5 petals, 5 pistils, and 5 stamens in the flower of the plant, or multiples thereof.

That's what made it a Rose! It is one of the largest families in the plant world. Every plant in that family has that characteristic. The flowering and the seeds of the plant are their reproductive system. That is a good place to begin classification of the plant family—a major characteristic.

With this in mind, look at the activities that are going on in a dividend-paying whole life insurance policy. Isn't it obvious that the insurance company must put lots of money to work in various places in order to be able to pay the death benefit, regardless of when the Insured dies? Isn't it also obvious that the Policy Owner outranks everyone in access to the pool of money (his equity in the policy) that must be lent? Isn't it obvious, too, that your need for financing the things of life is greater—during your lifetime—than your need for death benefit? This is not true with Term Life Insurance because most such policies never pay a death benefit because the insured only keeps the policy for a limited time frame. Therefore, the insurance company doesn't have to collect much premium in order to pay the death benefit for those who do happen to die during the limited time frame.

So, if I had been given the job on naming the product that Life Insurance companies came up with (Whole Life Insurance), I would have called it, "**A Personal Warehouse of Wealth System, With a Death Benefit As a Bonus.**" That's a rather long name, so we would have had to come up with an acronym of some kind, but it would have been far more accurate—and we wouldn't have all the confusion that exists today.

2

LOOKING AT A LIFE INSURANCE POLICY OVER A LONG PERIOD OF TIME

How you *think* is everything! Most people don't think long range.

After 10 years of working as a consulting forester, working in the life insurance industry as an agent for 35 years, and lecturing on the subject of life insurance for an additional 12 years, plus purchasing lots of life policies beginning when I was age 13, it is evident to me that people just don't look at the performance of a dividend-paying whole life policy over a long enough period of time. They only consider the results during the first few years—say, 10 years at the longest. Such a policy is engineered to get better, every day, as long as the policy is in force. The earlier one starts, the longer one continues, the better the policy gets.

Since I was educated as a forester, I tend to think about things over a much longer period of time, something like 70 years. I'm not going to be here that far in the future, and you probably won't either. But, I see nothing wrong with *thinking* that way. Plan as if you are going to live forever—but, live as if you are going to die today sounds like a good idea.

Take a look at the results of the last 20 years of a policy I bought from State Farm Life in 1959 to adjust your own perspective. I bought this policy from my brother, a State Farm Agent, while I was a Forester in North Carolina.

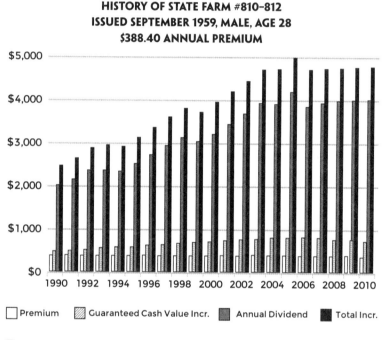

Figure 2. History of Existing State Farm Policy

At the time of this writing, the policy is 52 years old. That's about one-fourth of the time that whole life insurance has been in existence. The bars on the graph represent the ***actual performance*** on a *year-to-year* basis. That is, you are not looking at *cumulative* results at any one point on the graph. For instance, in 1990 I paid $388.40 premium. The Guaranteed Cash Value *increase*, that year, was $500.00. The dividend, that year, was $2,000.00. The *total increase* in cash value was

$2,500.00. The increases for each of the following years were *added to the values of the preceding years*.

Now, let's "fast-forward" and look at the year 2005. Notice that the Guaranteed Cash Value increased $800.00 and the dividend was $4,200.00 resulting in a $5,000.00 total increase that year. Of course, all I paid that year was $388.40.

The $388.40 premium doesn't sound like much money to you—but, a 28 year old in 1959 who was making $10,000 per year was "above the average bear." So, that premium in proportion to my income was a pretty significant matter. I'll bet that my brother bragged to his peers for a couple of months about what he had sold me!

Notice that the dividend now is *ten times the premium*. It would have been *twelve times* the premium had I not used dividends for the first fifteen years of the policy to reduce the premiums! You see, I was looking at the policy the way most everyone looks at life insurance—"you want to pay as little premium as possible and get as much death benefit for that little outlay"—therefore, use the increasing dividends to reduce the premium each year. **That's the way I thought!** After living with this limited understanding of the dynamics of dividend-paying whole life insurance for fifteen years, it finally dawned on me that I should be using the annual dividend to *buy paid-up additional insurance!* So, I changed the dividend election to purchase paid-up insurance (at no cost)—from that year on. Someone should have told me to do that at the very beginning! By the way, this change of dividend election was not dependent upon my insurability at the time of the election. I *directed* the insurance company to make the change.

To understand this next point we need to take a little "side trip" to better understand the economic world. I have been passionately studying Austrian Economics for 55 years and I know that the dollar has lost 80% of its purchasing power in the last 50 years. That fact can be substantiated by any number of economists. The Federal Reserve System has been inflating the money supply so much that it now takes $5.00 to buy what $1.00 would buy in 1959.

My own experience confirms this. In 1953 I remember buying chicken breast at the commissary at March Air Force Base, California for $1.00 per pound. Because of Mr. Greenspan—and now, Mr. Bernanke—inflating the money supply (they have weakened the power of the dollar), chicken breast should cost $5.00 per pound to be equal today. It does not!

The *real* cost has gone *down*! Yet most folks think that the price has gone up because "the numbers" have increased.

While in college in 1949 I worked in a produce store, part time. Bananas cost 16 cents per pound. Because of inflation bananas should sell for 80 cents per pound now. They don't. The highest prices I've seen are 69 cents. Bananas have gone down in cost. Just this week, I bought them for 44 cents at Costco.

We have three children. The first two were born while I was in the military. Our youngest is our only "civilian-born baby." The room rent at the hospital in Smithfield, NC in 1960 was $16.00 per day. Incidentally, the Holiday Inn Motel in that area at that same time frame was $16.00 per day!!! I travel a great deal on speaking engagements all over the United States and quite often will stay at Hampton Inns. As an average, the room rent, nationwide, is about $80.00 per night. (Plus, you get breakfast!). So, the only difference between 1960 and now is the inflation factor of "5." It takes $5.00 now to do what $1.00 did back then.

As further aside, let's talk about the current rates for hospital room rent. My Mother-in-law died over four years ago.

She was in skilled nursing for three years. From time to time she had to go to the hospital. The last time she went, the room rent at the hospital was $1,500 per day. What happened to the "five-factor?" It disappeared on account of two things—the introduction of "third party payers" (insurance companies) and government programs. A third party payer removes the normal abrasion of the market place. In essence, the provider of service says, "You don't need to worry yourself about the cost—*the insurance company* is going to pay it!" They neglect to explain what that does to premium costs. Now, multiply this by ten—or more—for the introduction of a government program and you get what's going on in America now.

As a result, the costs of health, education and welfare have all gone up significantly above the "five-factor"while the *actual cost* of everything else has gone down. In 1964 the average cost of a year in college at a state school was $2,000.00 per year. Now, it is ten to twenty times as much.

The common denominator in this current situation is the fact people have abdicated their responsibility/opportunity of building their own Warehouse of Wealth and have turned the function over to the bankers. And the bankers have made them slaves! This should have never happened.

Please note that health, education and welfare are all items in which the government is now heavily involved. It wasn't always that way and we all lived very well. The Department of HEW should never have come into existence.

Finally, I rode American Airlines a great deal in 2001. The Flight Magazine in the pouch in front of your seat was celebrating its 30th anniversary. There were several articles about "then, and now." Costs of many items were cited—and they all met the "five-factor" perfectly. Assuming that you are convinced of the validity of the "five-factor" I can now tell you that the death benefit of this policy in 1959 was $20,000. The death benefit now is over $100,000. It has kept up with inflation perfectly! Have you ever heard anyone say that life insurance was a hedge against inflation? Not on your life! To the contrary, they say it is a *victim* of inflation. Yet, these folks don't know very much about how this type of life insurance actually works—but they are sharing their ignorance with those who will listen. Coupled with the fact that I have been putting in dollars each year that have been *depreciating in value.* The value of the dollar I paid this year is only 20% of the one I paid in 1959.

When I paid the premium on this policy in 2005 I directed State Farm Life to *change the dividend election* for the year 2006 and all following years—send the annual dividend *check to me. (I don't need the income—but I wanted to be able to show the dividend* check to those non-believers).

The check for 2006 was $3,877.70, for 2007 it was $3,927.28, for 2008 it was $3,973.33, for 2009 it was $4,015.55.

So, let's do some basic arithmetic—take the annual premium ($388.00) per year and multiply by the number of years the policy has been in force (52). That is my *gross outlay.* Now, subtract the value of the dividends I used to reduce premiums the first fifteen years. We have now isolated my *net cost of the policy to date (my cost basis for the policy).*

These dividend checks have all been tax-free because they equal what I have paid into the policy over the years up to that point. In July of 2010 I got a letter from State Farm requesting that I furnish my Social Security Number to make sure their records were correct, because I had recovered all the cost basis of the policy—therefore, all the dividend checks in the future would be *taxable.* I responded by directing them to *change the*

Figure 3. Actual State Farm Dividend Checks

dividend election back to purchasing paid-up additional insurance (again, this was done regardless of my insurability). *Before* one recovers cost-basis, the dividends aren't a taxable event because they are a return of premium. But then, after recovering cost-basis, it's no longer a return of premium since you've already gotten all of your premiums back. The reason dividend PUAs aren't taxable from this time forward, is because they are buying more insurance.

I can get this kind of income, tax free, *for the rest of my life if I make a policy loan* of $4,000 per year—and the net death benefit will not diminish!!!! That's because the dividends are purchasing increasing amounts of death benefit faster than the increasing policy loan.

I think you will admit that this is an impressive result. But, the *very impressive* factor is not seen! I was a pilot in the Alabama Army National Guard in 1971. One of my fellow pilots got "between the rock and a hard place" financially and needed to raise some money.

He knew I was educated as a Forester and might be interested in buying the 100 acres of timberland he owned in northwest Alabama. He said, "I'll sell it to you for $50.00 per acre—and I will finance it for you for ten years." I knew that was a good deal and took it—and made monthly payments to him. This was not a speculative venture—it was property that I knew something about. Remember, I'm educated as a Forester and worked in that field for ten years.

About 18 months later he called me again and requested that we get together to talk. He said, "I underestimated my need for cash. If you will just pay off the debt on that land now, I will discount it 25 cents on the dollar." I knew that was a good deal so I replied, "Stand real still—I'll be right back." I went directly to the regional State Farm office and said, "Get me a $3,500 policy loan quickly before this young man changes his mind!" In less than an hour I had a check in his hand.

Bottom line—I had less than $38.00 per acre invested in that land. In 1985 I sold that land for $500.00 per acre—and I financed it for 10 years at 15% interest! With that income I bought more life insurance. All those premiums become cost basis in the new policy and I will get it back, tax free, when I decide to draw "passive income" (dividends) from it.

During the following years I made two more investments from policy loans on this policy. They results were not quite this good—but, they were highly profitable. These facts are not seen as you look at the graph. You have to add these results to what is shown on the graph to understand the total power of dividend-paying whole life insurance. This is what *Building Your Warehouse of Wealth* is all about. You have almost immediate access to money to take advantage to opportunities that will surely appear. In fact, if you have a readily available pool of cash, opportunities will "track you down."

> *Does having money safe and available when you*
> *need it take away any of your options?*
>   —BILL LENDERMAN

Out in the big, wide world there are those who say, "But, those dividends are not guaranteed." Let's look at the facts. Once per year the Directors of the insurance company meet and declare what the *dividend scale* for the next year will be. This is allocated to all the policies on an equitable basis. It *is guaranteed for the next year!*

It cannot go backward like your Enron Stock, your WorldCom Stock, your Global Crossings Stock, etc. The only dividends that are not guaranteed are those in the future beyond that point.

If you elect to have the annual dividend to buy additional paid-up insurance—at no cost—and regardless of your health condition at that time—what you have is an ever-compounding increase in cash value with no tax consequences.

Now, go back and study the graph of this policy. Note the dividend in 1990. There was a precipitous drop in interest rates that year, but notice that the dividend the following year went up! In 1992 it went up again. It leveled off in 1993, and went down slightly in 1994 and then continued its upward trend. There were minor "corrections" in '99, '04 and '06, but the upward trend is evident.

I remind you that this policy has been in force since 1959. Since that time there have been all sorts of changes in interest rates. When I moved to Birmingham, AL in 1963, our mortgage rate on the house was 5¼% interest. If I wanted a new mortgage 20 years later, the rate would have been 16%! Now, we have been experiencing low interest rates for the past few years. This resulted in people increasing their debt and decreasing their savings. The net result—the "banking function became the province of the bankers" and the world-wide problem today is the unbelievable amount of debt.

Yet, with all these aberrations, this policy has been consistently improving. Question—do you think interest rates on house mortgages will remain this low? I think not. They are already beginning to increase significantly. Reality is settling in! The "fool's paradise" is coming to an end! *It always does.*

Shortly before I bought this policy from my brother, I was called upon by a representative of a financial services company (who shall remain nameless) who showed me a "mountain wave graph of lies" about how good I would have done in the stock market if I had put $10,000 into it twenty years before.

"Do you have $10,000 to put into such a plan today?" he asked. "No, I replied." He responded, "Don't worry about it—we have an accumulation plan in which you can put $50.00 per month ($600 per year) and, in time, it will become $10,000. At that time we can put it into one of our mutual funds and you will be set for life!" I indulged. The agent made me initial the point on his projection at which my outlay would equal its value. It was *eight years!*

So, I was paying $600.00 per year in that plan and $388.40 to the SF policy. That's $1,000 per year—10% of my income at the time. Remember, it was my next older brother that sold me the SF policy. He knew about the $600.00 that I was paying into the other plan. What if brother had suggested that I pay the entire $1,000.00 into the SF policy? Then, the dividend check that I am now receiving would be over $10,000.00 per year! And, I would have had more money in the interim years to take advantage of investments that would have come along. If, in this scenario, I had bought paid-up additional insurance with the dividends for *all the years* of this policy, then the dividend would have been $12,000 per year!

Furthermore, brother knew that I was running heavy equipment (Caterpillar tractors) to clear land for tree growing purposes in my business. I was paying a finance company $1,500.00 per month on heavy equipment.

That's $18,000.00 per year! Where did the finance company get the money to lend me? From insurance companies!! Finance companies buy "blocks" of money from insurance companies, fragment those blocks and sell the money to consumers, who agree to pay back the finance company monthly over a period of time, adding a higher interest rate, of course.

Brother should have taught me to pay $18,000.00 per year in life insurance premiums to accumulate a pool of capital from which, eventually, I could finance *all* my equipment. There was no way I could do that *immediately* since my income was $10,000.00 per year. But, he could have sold me, say 4 times the amount that he did, and in a few years I could have been rid of one of those tractor payments forever.

I could have been making what the finance company was making off me, tax free, for the balance of my life. Once a person gets past the point of financing one item in his scenario, he can accelerate the process very quickly. In about 15 years, a business person can be **totally self-sufficient**. I know of one case where a business owner "got rid of the banks" in only three and one-half years and the amount of the payoff was over $500,000.

Question: Why didn't brother teach me these things? Answer: He didn't know. Question: Why didn't he know? Answer: State Farm Life didn't teach him!

Well, why didn't they teach him? All because of how they **thought!** All the qualities of dividend-paying whole life insurance that *Infinite Banking Concepts* teaches have been there for 200 years!

Brother died on the first day of January 1981 at age 52. I'm 81 at this point in time, so, in the not too distant future I will be reunited with him in the hereafter. This earthly existence is simply "training camp for the eternal."

When we get over the pleasantries of meeting again, then I'm going to have a serious discussion with him about this matter. "Why didn't you sell me much more life insurance than you did?"

A question comes to mind—do you think Dave Ramsey or Suze Orman have a clue about this type of dividend-paying whole life insurance? I don't think so, but they are making the "big bucks" on TV and otherwise "bad-mouthing" Whole Life Insurance.

3

SPENDING HABITS OF AMERICANS

S ome analogies are helpful at this point—look at the globe in this figure.

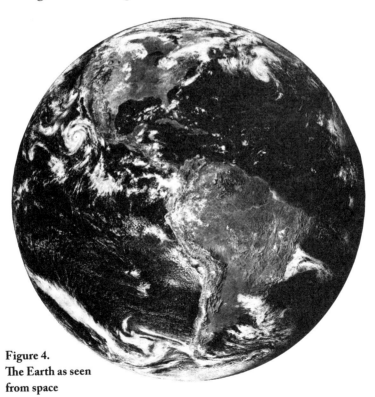

Figure 4.
The Earth as seen
from space

Isn't it obvious that about 80 percent of the earth's surface is water? The sun heats up that surface and some of it will evaporate into the atmosphere. Warm air rises because it is lighter. Moist air is lighter than dry air, also. So, warm, moist air is really lighter! This will cause wind currents that take the moisture around the earth. From time to time that moisture will precipitate out as rain, sleet and snow and hail. And some of it will pass through you and me. We can't live without water.

When it passes through us, it will eventually end up back in the oceans. It is a cycle. All bodies of water are connected in some manner or another. It might be just in the form of moisture in the air. This *flow* of water is necessary for us to live. We don't just drink water one time and that's it!

Similarly, there is only one pool of money in the world. The fact that the pool is being managed by various banks, insurance companies, corporations, and individuals and in various currency denominations and countries is incidental. The money in your wallet or purse is part of the banking system.

When you go to buy something money must *flow* from you to the seller in a relatively short period of time, otherwise nothing happens. If money didn't flow it would be worthless.

When money flows it ultimately ends up back in the Warehouse of Wealth. Without the concept of warehousing our money we would all be on a barter system. We would be "back in the caves." Someone is going to perform the Warehouse of Wealth function. *How much of this function do you control as it relates to your needs in life?*

Everyone needs a heart and it must be working, otherwise we can refer to you in the past tense. The heart is both a reservoir of blood and it is a pump. It pumps the blood to wherever it is needed through arteries and then returns it through veins back to the heart after it has been rejuvenated by the other organs. But, have you ever considered the fact that you could live without a non-functioning heart? I did—for about two and one-half hours some 24 years and three months ago. The heart surgeons had mine outside the chest cavity while re-plumbing four coronary arteries. During this time my heart was not working. The surgery team shut it down. Yet, here I am writing this book. What made this possible? A wonderful machine called a heart-lung machine. It did everything my heart was doing—but only marginally so.

Water has got to *flow*. Blood has got to *flow*. Money has got to *flow*. With these three analogies I'm going to demonstrate that in the financial world most folks are doing the equiva-lent of living on a heart-lung machine nearly 35 percent of the time. Absurd! They should never have to be on the machine!

Let's go back to Figure 1—How a Participating Whole Life Insurance Policy works shown on page 7. Study it for a few minutes.

With the information we have seen so far, how are human beings actually behaving in this possible financial environment?

Several years ago I did a good bit of study on the spending habits of American families. Through the years I have kept an eye on the figures and the proportion of income allocated to each category. I suggest that you do your own study of this pat-tern of spending and draw your own conclusions. This seems to be the current situation, and doesn't really change all that much over the lifetime of individuals. I build scenarios around the "All- American family" because I don't want people to think you have to be rich to create a banking system that can handle all your needs for finance. This young man is 29 years old and is making $28,500 per year after taxes. What does he do with the after-tax income?

Annual Pattern of Spending

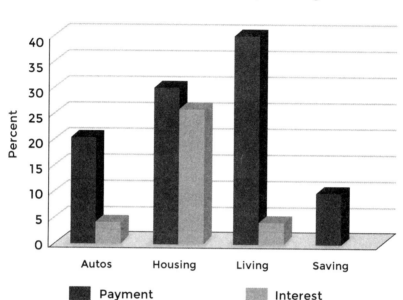

Figure 5. Annual Pattern of Spending Habits

Twenty percent is spent on transportation, thirty percent is spent on housing, forty-five percent is spent on "living" (clothes, groceries, contributions to religious and charitable causes, boat payments, casualty insurance on cars, vacations, etc.) Many of these items are financed by credit cards or bank notes. The balance is *financed* by paying cash for them—and thus, giving up interest that could be earned, otherwise. He is saving less than five percent of disposable income.

But, to be as generous as possible, let's assume that he is saving *ten percent* and spending only forty percent on living expenses. This is giving him every benefit of the doubt on the matter of savings. Just remember, the real situation is at least twice as bad as what is depicted!

The problem is that all these items are *financed* by other banking organizations. An automobile *financing* package (this is *not* the cost of the car—it is how much is financed) for this hypothetical person is $10,550 for 48 months with an interest rate of at least 8.5% with payments of $260.05 per month. But, if you will check with the sales manager of an automobile agency you will find that 95% of the cars that are traded in *are not paid for!* (Don't take my word for this, do your own research on this matter—call on the owner, or sales manager of a number of car dealers and ask them that question).

This means, at the end of 30 months, if the car is traded, 21% of every payment dollar is *interest.* Even if he goes the full four years, the portion of every payment made is still 20%! This means that the interest portion of every dollar spent is perpetual. It never seems to dawn that the *volume of interest* is the real issue, not the *annual percentage rate.* For a real thrill, go to see the sales manager of the high priced cars and ask him what percentage of the cars that leave their car lot are *leased.* The answer will probably be 75%, or more! This is worse than financing a car purchase.

When you go to the Doctor's office to get a shot of some kind, the criteria is not the *rate* at which the medicine is injected into you—it is the *volume!* Too little, and it won't do any good—too much and it can kill you!

Now, let's move to the housing situation. This young man can qualify for a 30 year fixed-rate mortgage in the amount of about $93,000 at a fixed interest rate of 7% APR with payments of $618.75 and closing costs of some $2,500.

The problem is that within 5 years he will move to another city, across town, or refinance the mortgage. Something happens to a mortgage within 5 years. Including the closing costs and interest paid out during these 60 months he had paid

$39,625, but only $5,458 has gone to reduce the loan. This means that $34,167 has gone to interest and closing costs. Divide the amount paid out into the interest and closing costs and you find that *86% of every dollar paid out goes to the cost of financing!*

If he sells the house in less than 5 years, the results are worse. This proportion never gets any better because he takes on a new mortgage and starts all over again. He thinks that he is "buying" a house, but all he is really doing is making the wheels of the banking business and the real estate business—in that order—turn. Again, don't take my word for this either—do your own research and prove this fact for yourself.

The amazing thing is that government leaders and financial organizations refer to the above paragraph as "home ownership!" All of this activity is simply making the wheels of the real estate business and the banking business turn! Absurd!

Today there are countless families that owe more on the house than it is worth—all because of this notion that "everyone should own a home." I wonder where that idea came from. Mortgage rates have decreased to ridiculous levels and induced people into buying houses that they cannot afford. The net effect of this action has turned the banking function over to the bankers and they have painted the American citizens into the worst corner of all time. The banking function should be controlled at the "you and me" level. It can be done through Building Your Warehouse of Wealth.

In the next segment of his spending pattern—the living expenses—you will find that the interest on his boat payments, credit card interest, plus the cost of casualty insurance on the automobiles, etc. will rival in volume the interest he is paying on the two automobiles. (Later on in this book you will learn how to self-insure for comprehensive and collision insurance on automobiles).

Now, add up all the interest he is paying out and you find that 34.5 cents of every disposable dollar paid out is *interest*. For the average All-American male this proportion *never changes*. Let's assume that he is trying to save 10% of his disposable income, *which is twice the average savings rate in America at this time*.

That means that we have a 3.45 to 1 ratio of interest paid out as compared to savings. If you will get this young man together with his peers at a coffee break or some such gathering and have one of them suggest that they discuss financial matters, I can predict what they will talk about—getting a *high rate of return* on the portion they are saving! Meanwhile, every participant in the conversation is doing the above! What a tragedy! But that is how they have learned to conduct their financial affairs. All because of the way they think! The banking industry has taught them well!

PROFESSIONAL CREDENTIALS

Down through the years it is very evident that "men love to have letters after their names:" PhD, MBA, MD, CPA, etc, etc. We are discussing the idea of Life Insurance here. In this business the first designation to appear was Chartered Life Underwriter (CLU). This designation is awarded to people who have passed a regimen of study that typically takes two years. At least, that's how long it took me. It is very equivalent to a Master's Degree at any college.

The American College, a private college in Bryn Mawr, Pennsylvania, offers the Chartered Life Underwriter curriculum and designation. Founded by the American College of Life Underwriters in the 1920s by **Solomon S. Huebner** of the University of Pennsylvania **Wharton School**, the CLU® was the first credential program offered. Dr. Huebner, as an early analyst of **human life value** and an **economic theory** educator, developed the first professional curriculum for insurance agents.

The human life value thought goes something like this: How old are you now? How many years do you expect to work? During this time frame, how much money, on an average, do you feel that you will earn per year? Multiply that number of years times your expected average income. That is your expected earnings during your working life. But, you will use up 40% of that income just to sustain yourself, your charities, your taxes, etc.

The 60% balance is what you are worth to your family, your charities, and others that you may care about. But, that is in the form of income over that period of time. To arrive at a principal sum that would produce that income over this period of time we must discount this figure at a nominal rate of interest. That figure, we will say, is $500,000. That is your **human life value.** Suppose that you owned a machine of some kind worth $500,000 and it was guaranteed to produce your income to your beneficiaries, but it was subject to destruction, total loss, etc., would you insure it? How much would you insure it for?

Now that we have that figure established, let me show you how little you will have to pay my company to guarantee that result. That was Dr. Huebner's contribution to the subject of life insurance to help people arrive at the amount of it that one should buy.

With this in mind, please go back and look at the Figure 5 –Graph of Annual Spending Habits on page 30. This typical person is spending 34.5 cents out of every dollar he spends on interest alone—and this pattern really doesn't change all that much during his entire lifetime. This tells you that his need for "finance" during his lifetime is huge!

Now, go back to Figure 1—How a Participating Whole Life Insurance Policy works on page 7. Let's correlate the graph with the diagram. It should be pretty obvious that his "need for finance during his life time" is greater than his "need for death benefit." When a policy owner pays a premium for life insurance, isn't it obvious that the company has to put it to work in order to be able to pay the ultimate death benefit? Isn't it also obvious that the Owner out-ranks all the possible places that the company must put the money to work?

Then, why not solve for the need for finance through this magnificent financial device? The reason that very few folks see this possibility is because of **the way they think.** They pay "pennies" in premiums and thus, have access to "pennies" in cash value and conclude, "Life Insurance is just a 'penny-ante' product." Nonsense! Change the way you think! **Put in large premiums**.

In due course, you have access to a **large pool of cash values** that are accessible for the major purchases in life through policy loans. Please remember that "it is all borrowed money." You finance everything you buy, whether you recognize the fact or not. Remember, also, that when you make a loan at a bank or some other financial organization, **you must pay it back**! When you buy life insurance from this type of company, **you own the contract**—not the company.

Do you want to steal from your Warehouse of Wealth and destroy it? I hope not. In fact, if you are half-way smart, you should pay the policy loan back at a higher rate of interest than what the company charges.

This extra money is just "additional capital" to expand your system. This is done through something called a "paid-up additions rider" or through buying additional policies.

I wonder why Dr. Huebner, at the American College didn't see this fact. Surely, it was because of **the way he thought.**

CONSIDER MY OWN PREVIOUS SPENDING HABITS

I spent 35 years in life insurance sales. Remember, also, that I was educated as a Forester and spent 10 years working in that arena. I thought that timberland was a good place to build and store wealth. (It is. A number of pension plans own vast amounts of timberland). So, I accumulated about 1,000 acres of such in Alabama and Georgia utilizing the All-American plan of acquisition—OPM—other people's money. As long as I stuck to this type of investment—something that I knew about—I made some money. But, the lure of all the magazine stories and other sources of how profitable it is to be involved in land-development with the use of leverage cast its snare.

You guessed it! I indulged. In the late '70s, I made some money that way, too. Prime interest rates at the local commercial banks at that time were 8% on 90-day loans.

But, I'm not a "prime customer"—that's the rate they charge their best customers—the ones they *know* they are going to get the money back. We used to be able to say that is like General Motors. Can't say that anymore—it is "Government Motors" now!

At every seminar that I conduct, I take a survey to see if there any "prime rate at a bank" people attending. Never met one yet! All of us peons have to pay 1½% over prime rate!

Nevertheless, I made some money under those conditions. Then along came 1980 and 1981. Prime rate rose to 21.5% and stayed there for 18 months. Add 1.5% to that and you have 23% interest.

I got caught owing a lot of money under those conditions. Through many months of this financial pain during that time, it finally dawned on me that I could make policy loans from three different life insurance companies at 5%, 6%, and 8%—and the only thing that limited how much I could borrow was the cash value in them. Although I had bought a lot of this type of insurance, it was nowhere near the amount I should have bought to solve this problem. I had been thinking the way most folks think!

Now I saw clearly that I should increase my premium outlay dramatically to more than six times my precious amount. This would create significant cash values from which I would borrow and pay off "the snakes and dragons" at the bank. When I described this idea to my peers in the life insurance business at that time, they all said, "You have a good idea there, but you owe a lot of money. As soon as you pay off your loans you should put your idea to work." Nope! That is the way the "world" thinks—and they have never been right about anything!

> *Enter through the narrow gate. For wide is the gate and broad is the road that leads to destruction, and many enter through it. But small is the gate and narrow the road that leads to life, and only a few find it.*
>
> —Matthew 7:13–14

Find a way to get the Warehouse of Wealth started as soon as possible. It can't be done overnight. It must be done incrementally. The earlier one starts a policy, the longer it is in force, the more efficient it gets.

The best time to plant a tree is 20 years ago. The next best time is today. Anonymous

4

TAX-QUALIFIED RETIREMENT PLANS

H ow you think is everything! Most people let their government do their thinking for them. Why?

Back in 2000 I wrote *Becoming Your Own Banker—The Infinite Banking Concept* and in it I briefly addressed the subject of retirement plans and specifically *Tax Qualified Retirement Plans.* Since that time it has become more apparent to me that this idea needs to be addressed more fully. Americans have become increasingly dependent on an idea that is defective and won't work. Basically, it is a Socialist idea and history has proved conclusively that Socialism won't work.

There is a fundamental reason for this fact that most people fail to recognize. To make my position on this subject perfectly clear let me state that, as of this writing, I am 81 years old. I have been a Christian since age 9 and have studied the Bible through and through during these years. I have also studied, with a passion, the teachings of the "Austrian" school of economics for over 55 years. From this background it is very evident to me that *all government programs* are nothing more than a manifestation of *man trying to play god, in the pagan sense of the word.* The book of Exodus in the Bible tells you that *God is a jealous God.* (Exodus 20:5) He won't put up with such efforts by man trying to displace Him in the order of things.

All government programs are initiated under the guise of "helping" citizens—when the real object is to control their lives. There is always the "hidden agenda" that is never stated. And Americans swallow the apparent immediate benefit, never realizing that there is a hook in that bait. In fact, as a student of Austrian Economics, if you give me the mission statement of any government plan I can predict, in due course, the eventual outcome with absolute certainty. As Shakespeare said, "[The] Truth will out." Just give it enough time. But man sees things over a very short time span as compared with that of God. His time table and ours are different.

All such efforts by man eventually fail—but they do so over a long enough time frame that man does not see it happening to him. He is subject to the "boiled frog syndrome." Put a frog in water his temperature and he is comfortable. Add a tiny bit of heat and he is still comfortable. He gets used to it. Add a tiny bit more and he is still comfortable, etc. Keep that process up and you can boil him! Now, I don't know whether that is true or not, but it is a great word picture of what has happened in the economic world of America. There are countless analogies that prove this point.

Another object of this writing is to demonstrate that we live in a world of lies! Everywhere we turn we are confronted with lies to the point of not being able to recognize this fact. John Stossel wrote a book in the recent past entitled *Myths, Lies and Downright Stupidity—Why Everything You Know Is Not True,* in which he demonstrates this truth. Napoleon Bonaparte is credited with the observation, "History is lies agreed upon."

Just a few days after September 11, 2001 Stephen Yates, a Philosophy Professor affiliated with the Ludwig von Mises Institute wrote an article on LewRockwell.com about a book he had read earlier that year where the two authors had predicted that something like 9/11 was going to occur somewhere about that time frame—give or take a couple of years on either side—that would change the world forever. Has the world changed since that time? Unless you are a "boiled frog" just *look* at what is happening all around you. Try taking a trip in an airplane. The world had changed significantly! All kinds of nonsense is going on under the supposed mission of *protecting us.*

The authors pointed out, go back 70 (+/−) years and you have The Great Depression. The world changed and has never been the same. Go back another 70 (+/−) years and you have The War of Northern Aggression—known to some as The Civil War.

That was no civil war—a civil war is when two or more factions fight for control of a country. Jeff Davis, et al, in the South had no designs on taking over Washington, D.C. and running this country, no more than George Washington, et al, had in taking over London, England some 70+ years earlier.

To the contrary, in both cases—they *wanted to get away* from the oppression of outrageous taxation! But, there is the ever-present hidden agenda that can be exposed only by historians who look deeply enough in the archives to ferret out the truth—more evidence of the fact that we live in a world of lies.

At that time the United States lived under a tax system of tariffs on manufactured goods. The South was an agricultural economy and the North was based on manufacturing. As a result 85% of the taxes were being paid by the South. Would you guess where the money was being spent? In the North, of course! If you lived in the South and were the least bit conscious of what was really going on, you would probably be a bit ticked off at this situation.

The taxes were being spent on corporate welfare—railroads, canals, internal improvements. The platform on which Lincoln ran for election was *a high tariff, internal improvements, and a central bank.* Henry Clay was Lincoln's idol and he labeled it The American System. It was a mercantilist economic plan based on the "American School" ideas of Alexander Hamilton, expanded upon later by Friedrich List, consisting of a high tariff to support internal improvements such as road-building, and a national bank to encourage productive enterprise and form a national currency. This program was intended to allow the United States to grow and prosper, by providing a defense against the dumping of cheap foreign products, mainly at the time from the British Empire

That so-called Civil War was not about slavery—it was about taxation. Read Tom DiLorenzo's book, *The Real Lincoln.* Read his follow-up book, *Lincoln Unmasked.* Read Charles Adams' book, *When in the Course of Human Events.* Read *Forced Into Glory* by Lerone Bennet, Jr.. Read *Lincoln Uber Alles: Dictatorship Comes to America* by John Avery Emison. Finally, read *Emancipating Slaves, Enslaving Free Men: A History of the American Civil War* by Jeffrey Rogers Hummel.

When you have finished these books you will *begin* to see more clearly the hidden agenda that is ever present in any government activity.

Go back another 70 + years and you have the so-called "Revolutionary War." A better classification would be "The War of Secession" from the mother country of England by thirteen independent colonies on account of "outrageous taxes." Studies that I have read reported that taxes were about

2% in the South and 1% in the North. Our Forefathers went to war over that for ten years. And, today we call nearly 50% "freedom!!" If our Forefathers could be re-incarnated today, they would go ballistic! "What have you people done?"

Continuing with the train of thought by Stephen Yates— go back another 70+ years—I have forgotten what happened. Then go back another 70+ years—I forgot that one, too. But the pattern is there! You can count on it—every 70 years or so something significant happens that changes the world in which we live.

So, I e-mailed Stephen immediately and brought to his attention that the Soviet Union came apart after 70 years. In my book, *Becoming Your Own Banker* I had predicted back in 1976 that Social Security would fail. Before it fails they will attempt to prop it up. The source of funds they will use is reserves on private pension plans, HR-10 plans, IRA's, et al.

People laughed at me, but in less than a year the first "trial balloon" went up, recognizing that this is possible. And now, it is common knowledge. In early October 2008 the incoming administration had personnel discussing confiscation of all such plans and combining them into a Guaranteed Retirement Account, or some name like that, and to be administered by Social Security. See how the "boiled frog" syndrome works? One small deviation from tried and true principle and people become comfortable with it. It becomes "normal." This leads to another deviation, etc., etc. etc. In due time it will lead to a complete U-turn in behavior and acceptance. The Constitution of the United States is a perfect example.

It started out based upon some rather good principles, but now I'm sure that at least 90% of what goes on in Washington, D.C. has no basis in the Constitution at all. And people just stand there and take it!

Anyway, Social Security in the U.S. started in 1937. Do the math. We are overdue. Any day now it will self-destruct. But the easiest thing the government can get to in order to try to keep the Ponzi scheme alive is to confiscate the reserves on all the other tax qualified plans. It is the largest block of securities in the world and so it will be irresistible to government authorities.

And for you Bible scholars, in the Old Testament the Israelite nation ended up back in slavery. In the book of Jeremiah he predicted they would be there for 70 years. They were only there for 68 years—but that's close enough for government work! You will see more about this is a later chapter of this book.

All the tax qualified retirement plans are a function of the IRS Code—which has only been around since 1913. The world got along very well before income tax. We had surpluses in the national budget before then.

Wise men told us what would happen when a country gets in income tax—and we see the results in spades now! Be sure and read *The Income Tax—Root of All Evil* by Frank Chodorov.

Before World War II there weren't many pension plans. According to the Congressional Budget Office website (www.cbo.gov/) The Revenue Acts of 1921, 1926, and 1928 initiated tax advantages for employment-based retirement plans. By 1929, about 15 percent of private-sector employees were covered by employment-based plans, which were concentrated in large corporations and in sectors in which government oversight tended to be the strongest.

And, then along comes WWII. I was a teenager at that time and very aware of what life was like. When you went to buy gasoline in those days it did not matter how much money you had—the limiting factor was—do you have an A, B or C sticker on your windshield of your car.

A bureaucrat in Washington knew how much gasoline you needed. This is an emergency! We have a war going on! Never mind that we had no business being involved in that war. For a starter on this subject read *Churchill, Hitler, and "The Unnecessary War"—How Britain Lost Its Empire and the West Lost the World* by Patrick J. Buchanan. Then read *The New Dealer's War* by Thomas Fleming. And *The Roosevelt Myth* by John T. Flynn. Also, *The Pearl Harbor Myth* by George Victor.

More evidence that *we live in a world of lies.* And we conduct our lives on the basis of that erroneous understanding.

When the housewife went to the grocery store in those days, it did not matter how much money she had. The limiting factor was another form of money called "ration points" and even with both these items she could only buy so much meat, so much butter, so much of this, so much of that. Everything was controlled! Frozen! A Socialist paradise! This was the genesis of the thought pattern that dominates American citizens today.

It has increased in its acceptance and today, we live in a Fascist nation—nominal title to property, but controlled in what we can do with it by our government. In time to come, it will not work! History proves the fact.

And so were wages. You could not give anyone a raise! Well, under such restrictions, how does a business give an employee a raise without giving him a raise? Benefits, of course! This marked the *real* beginning of Retirement Plans and Health Plans, as we know them today that were tax qualified. It only applied to corporate employees. This is an *exception* to the IRS Code, which was adopted in 1913. The USA didn't declare war until December 1941. In 1950 Paul Poirot at the Foundation for Economic Education wrote an essay entitled, *The Pension Idea* in which he demonstrated conclusively that the idea would never work. And here we are, early in the 21st Century and we see corporate pension plans falling apart with increasing regularity.

After WWII sole proprietors and partners noticed that because of pension plans corporate employees had a tax advantage over them.

So appeal was made to the authorities, "We need a tax-break, too." The result was the creation of Keogh Plans (HR-10 plans). Initially, participants in this category could contribute $2,500 per year to such a plan. "The contribution will be taken off your income for tax purposes this year. It will build tax-free until your retirement age—and you are going to be in a lower tax bracket at that time!" Of course, when you look at the history of the IRS Code and all the changes that have taken place—and you can rest assured there *will be changes in the future*—none of them to your advantage. The sole proprietors and partners agitated more and the contribution limit was raised to $7,500 per year.

More time passed and the balance of the population said, in essence, "Wait a minute, you authorities have blessed the corporate employees with a tax-break, you have blessed the sole proprietors and partners with a tax-break—what about us? Give us a tax-break, too!"

And so, along comes Individual Retirement Accounts. How was the idea sold to Congress? The rationale went something like this—the savings rate among everyday Americans is decreasing—our capital base is eroding! If we will give these folks a tax-break then they will start saving more and we will solve this problem. Of course, the amount of the contribution was limited, too.

What was the result? The savings rate actually went down! Naturally! All you have to do to understand this phenomenon is watch this TV commercial in Birmingham, AL years ago by Jefferson Federal Savings & Loan. (By the way, they don't exist now, along with thousands of other savings & loan organizations). Ron Eason, their public relations man is sitting in a big easy chair, coffee mug in his hand before the blazing fireplace. He looks you squarely in the eye and asks, "How is your retirement plan doing? Mine is *fixed!* I have an IRA at Jefferson Federal Savings & Loan. Do you know that for as little as $10 per month you can start an IRA there.

Your contribution will be taken off your income for tax purposes this year and it will build tax-free until your retirement time, and you will be in a lower tax bracket at that time?" (LOL)

What did "Joe Six-Pack" conclude as a result of watching this commercial? He says to himself, "Wow! With a plan that good, I don't have to save *half as much as I did before!* I can take the difference and *make a down payment on a boat!*" And so, the savings rate went down. During that era, for two successive years, when I got my New York Life annual statement for premiums due, there was another letter from the president of the company explaining how the savings rate had gone down.

And so, following this chain of events—pension plans, then Keogh Plans, and finally IRAs and 401-Ks—now everyone has an *exception to the IRS Code!* All of these plans are a function of the IRS Code!

Consider then, this reasoning—when government creates a problem (onerous taxation) and then, turns around and grants you an exception to the problem *they created*—(any tax-qualified plan) aren't you just a little bit suspicious that you are being manipulated? All of these plans were introduced as a means of *helping* citizens out. If they really wanted to help, all they had to do is reduce the taxes! Do you really think they want to do that? The real object is to control your life! And you just stand there and willingly participate! What in the world has happened to the ability to think?

The first nine pages of the IRS Code describe income. The following 1,100 pages describe the *exceptions* to the code. In essence, the Code is saying, "We own everything but we will grant you these exceptions."

Does this help you to see the *hidden agenda* that is always there in any government program? The best way for them to accomplish this goal is to *make you dependent* on them for sustenance. There is a tremendous element of *dependence* in the act of worship. You will worship that on which you are *dependent*. They sell these mind-crippling ideas through the use of lies! It is all the result of how people think!

When people think that their blessings in life come from government, they will always end up in slavery!

Along this chain of thought—when I got out of the Air Force in 1954 and went to work in the civilian world did you know that Social Security did not apply to Farmers? It did not apply to Doctors, Lawyers, and Clergymen, either. One by one, they succumbed to the siren song of dependence on government.

As of the time of writing this book, students currently graduating from religious seminaries can opt out of Social Security. Years ago, when I was in the life insurance business I convinced three young seminary graduates to opt out and simply put what they would have to put into SS into high premium whole life insurance with a Mutual Life Insurance Company.

The results would be far better than any alternative. After several years of participating in my recommendation, all three fell by the wayside, victims of the siren song of government dependence. The deciding factor was the introduction of Medicare. When it came into existence it was tied to SS— one could not be covered for Medicare without being covered by SS. They just couldn't visualize life without Medicare! The world got along very well without SS, Medicare and hundreds of other government programs for years but the hidden agenda of government methodology combined with the "boiled frog" syndrome has plunged America into a one-way trip to disaster. All empires fail—and so will this one.

When Christian leaders (Clergymen, Pastors, and Church Leaders) don't understand the connection between the act of worship and the concept of dependence, isn't this a time of impending disaster? They claim to profess worshiping God but can't visualize life without a government program! Back them into a corner by suggesting that Social Security, for instance, be terminated and you will see who they *really worship*. Their behavior tells the truth of the matter. Americans are "captives in Egypt" in slavery and don't know it!

Once you take a handout from a government program, it does something to your mind. You can't think straight—and you become a slave.

In figure 6 you are looking at a graphical representation of a 1958 Commissioners Standard Ordinary Mortality Table—the pattern at which people died at that time. In constructing such tables Actuaries are dealing with a population of 10,000,000 *selected lives—people who have been through a screening process.* They have passed a physical exam and are judged to live until normal life expectancy. And, until recently they were dealing with a theoretical lifespan of 100 years.

The graph you see is extracted from that data. Out of the 1,000 born at that time, 10% were projected to die by age 45.

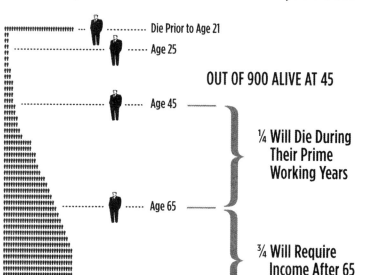

OUT OF 1,000 AMERICANS BORN . . . 1,000 DIE!

Die Prior to Age 21

Age 25

OUT OF 900 ALIVE AT 45

Age 45

¼ Will Die During
Their Prime
Working Years

Age 65

¾ Will Require
Income After 65

Age 80

¼ Will Require
Income After 80

Age 100

You are looking at the 1958 SCO Mortality Table

**Figure 6. More evidence to help you visualize why Social Security will
ultimately fail.**

Out of the remaining 900 twenty five percent were expected
to die by age 65. Seventy five percent were expected to die
after age 65. So, it is evident that most of the deaths occurred
after age 65.

Let's take time out here and examine where this *weird idea* of age 65 came from. The idea of *retirement* is a relatively recent concept. Nowhere in history is the word even mentioned, to any degree. I have studied the Bible through and through for many years and I can't find anywhere that ". . . so, Moses retired and lived happily thereafter." Basically the idea started in Germany about 1890 with Bismarck. These were the folks that gave the world the idea of retirement and government sponsored Social Security.

Bismarck set retirement age for German males at 70. In 1916 it was reduced to age 65. In 1890 life expectancy for Germans was about 45, so you see; it was probable that the average person would never collect anything. Anyway, this is where Roosevelt (FDR) got age 65 for our Social Security in 1937. At that time life expectancy for American males was about 61 years. Now it is about 78—and we have most people talking about *retiring* at age 65—or even less! Forget it! It can't happen!

I have read predictions of living to age 120 are possible due to increased technology. Life insurance companies now have policy plans of Life Paid-Up 121 years in view of this possibility. But, yet, there are people who hope to "retire early"—say age 55 or so.

"I'm going to work for 30 years and retire for 50 years." Get real! It can't work! A major change in the way people think is overdue.

I have read studies where it will take 80% of my grandchildren's income to supply Social Security income to their parent's generation. There is no way that can happen. It is impossible to do! It can't work!

Furthermore, I drew up the following scenario over 30 years ago and no one had the courage to repeat it. "Three men were born in the U.S. on the same day. One was Caucasian, one was Hispanic, and the third was Black. They all had similar jobs during their working life and hence paid maximum into the Social Security scheme. They all achieved retirement age and drew their first SS check. But, one month later the Black man died. It is a statistical fact that Blacks don't live as long as Hispanics and Caucasians. And those Japanese folks live even longer. You can pass all the laws you want to and you can't change that fact!

The next month the Black man's widow died. How many times have you heard reports of one spouse dying and the surviving spouse dies shortly thereafter? I read an extensive study recently about the effects of loneliness on longevity. It is real! What happened to all the money the Black man paid into SS all of his working life? The fact is it doesn't exist! That money has already been spent by the US government and worthless IOUs are put into a file in a cave in West Virginia. There is no money in the *SS Trust Fund!* The fallacious theory is that the program will continue by confiscations from future generations.

The following month the Hispanic man dies—and the month after that his widow dies. What happened to all the money he put into SS? Same thing—it doesn't exist! Lies don't last forever. One way or another truth will emerge.

The net result of the foregoing is that the money the Black man and the Hispanic man paid into SS goes to sustain the Ponzi scheme for a few more years for the benefit of the *White man's widow*—because they outlive the White men. Please tell me how long that scheme will last when everyone catches onto this fact!"

This is totally unfair and is a sterling example of the Law of Unintended Consequences that is the hallmark of every government program. They will never work because they are all manifestations of man trying to play god, in the pagan sense of the word. God is a jealous God. He won't put up with such nonsense. Will US Citizens ever learn!?

This is the verdict:

Light has come into the world, but men loved darkness instead of light because their deeds were evil.

—JOHN 3:19 NIV

5

INVESTMENTS OF TAX-QUALIFIED PLANS

Since WWII there has been an accelerating emphasis on Tax Qualified Retirement Plans. The contributions have to be put to work in investments of some kind. In the very recent years emphasis has been on 401-K plans (defined contribution plans) as opposed to the original Pension Plans (defined benefit plans) that are disappearing from the scene. What has been the universally recommended investment for these contributions? Why stocks or mutual funds, of course! They are always going to go up!

(Try reading *The Brainwashing of the American Investor* by Steven R. Selengut. Read *Eat The Rich* by P. J. O'Rourke. Read *Devil Take the Hindmost* by Edward Chancellor. Read *Inventing Money* by Nicholas Dunbar. But, above all read Barry J. Dyke's book, *The Pirates of Manhattan, II—Highway to Serfdom.*) These books will be a good start in understanding the lies that people believe and upon which they have based their financial future. It is really unbelievable what has happened in the financial world on account of fallacious economic thinking.

By the way, stocks are often referred to as "securities." I don't see anything that was secure about Enron, about WorldCom, about HealthSouth, about Long Term Capital Management, etc., etc., etc. The list could go on for several pages. How do these charlatans get away with such designations? Words have meaning. So their favorite strategy is to change the meaning of words. Boiled frogs feel more comfortable that way!

At the end of WWII there was a significant increase in birth rate in the US. A generation later there was a "birth dearth"—the birth *rate* went down. Demographers called this phenomenon a "pig in a python," a good word picture to demonstrate what is happening. A python is a large snake. Snakes don't chew things up—they swallow the victim whole. This creates a lump in their bodies and that lump moves along their digestive tract until it is absorbed over a period of time. Hence, this great word picture is used to describe the "Baby Boomers."

The first "Baby Boomer" turned 60 in October 2007. Go back and look at the graph in Figure 6. Do you see the "pig in a python" on a vertical plane? That data was for 1958. What has happened to "the pig" since that time? It has dropped significantly—or you could move the year 80 on the graph up to where 65 is located and you would have a pretty accurate picture of the situation today.

According to all Tax Qualified Plans, when one turns 70 ½ you *must* begin to take income (taxable) from your plan. That means you have to sell your stocks or mutual fund shares. Pray tell, who will you sell them to? Where are the buyers in the next generation? Furthermore, there is no way Americans can enjoy their present standard of living without the Chinese and Japanese buying our government bonds. When we buy their merchandise, we pay for it with our dollars. They have to do something with those dollars, so they buy our bonds. Years ago, Milton Friedman is credited with saying, "What could be more idyllic than the Japanese sending us high quality merchandise—and we send them worthless bits of paper in exchange?" Will they continue to be fools forever? I don't think so!

About ten years from now, there will be a large number of "baby boomers" *who will have to sell their stocks and mutual funds.* What happens to the value of these things when there are no buyers? All *HELL* is going to break loose in the economy at that time! Again, as of the time of this writing (early 2012), suppose that you had your retirement nest egg in stocks and mutual funds and you just turned 70 ½ in 2008. Great time to be selling, huh? Ten years from now is almost certain to be much worse! To help you understand this more fully, subscribe to Bill Bonner's stuff on www.dailyreckoning.com and read it every day. Better still, read *Financial Reckoning Day* by Bill Bonner and Addison Wiggin. Read their follow up book, *Empire of Debt.* Then read their latest, *Financial Reckoning Day Fallout.*

Bonner says, "We are at the beginning of a DEPRESSION—not a recession! The cure for a depression is a depression! The correction will be equal and opposite to the buildup." America has been living in a "fool's paradise" for about 50 years. Bonner says that "it will take 19 years to correct the economic nonsense that has accumulated during this time frame." Brace yourselves; there are some trying times ahead. Just imagine what it will be like if you have put your confidence in Tax-Qualified Retirement plans.

Surely, sometime in your life you have eaten corn on the cob during a meal. Have you ever counted the kernels on the cob? I did recently—it was over 500. Suppose you were a farmer and put a kernel of corn in the ground under favorable conditions. It produced a cornstalk with three ears of corn, each with about 500 kernels—the Law of the Harvest. So, one seed produced 1,500 kernels. Now, suppose you are going to be taxed by the government—on which would you rather be taxed—the seed or the harvest? Most every thinking person says, "The seed, of course." But, have you noticed that every Tax Qualified plan is predicated on the opposite? They all say, "Your contribution is taken off your income for tax purposes now—it will build tax-free until your retirement time—and you will be in a *lower tax bracket at that time.*" Ha! Ha! Ha! The IRS "suckered you in" again! It is all about how one thinks! And you let them do your thinking for you!

Lies! Lies! Lies! Americans have swallowed those lies for many years, but eventually reality sets in and there are all kinds of despair. Woe is us! What can be done? And they clamor for more government plans to rectify the disaster that was caused by the original government plans! Unbelievable!

> *There is nothing that is a more certain sign of insanity than to do the same thing over and over and expect the result to be different.*
>
> —Albert Einstein

Hopefully, this has helped you to see that government plans can't work. They are manifestations of "man trying to play god, in the pagan sense of the word." God is a jealous God (Exodus 20:5) and he won't put up with such nonsense. Does this help in recognizing the "boiled frog syndrome?" Governments promote their plans through the use of lies. But eventually, truth will out. Free people contracting with one another can solve all our financial and economic problems.

But, one has to recognize a lie when it shows up. All Tax Qualified Retirement plans need to be avoided like the plague—because they are!

SOME THINGS FOR YOU TO PONDER

The U.S. Post Service was established in 1775. The Government has had 237 years to get it right and it is BROKE.

Social Security was established in 1935. The Government has had 77 years to get it right and it is BROKE.

Fannie Mae was established in 1938. The Government has had 74 years to get it right and it is BROKE.

War on Poverty started in 1964. The Government has had 48 years to get it right; 1$ trillion of our money is confiscated each year and transferred to "the poor." They want MORE.

Medicare and Medicaid were established in 1965. The Government has had 47 years to get it right and they are BROKE.

Freddie Mac was established in 1970. The Government has had 42 years to get it right and it is BROKE.

The Department of Energy was created in 1977 to lessen our dependence on foreign oil. It has ballooned to 16,000 employees with a budget of $24 billion a year and we import more oil than ever before. The Government has had 35 years to get it right and it is an abysmal FAILURE.

The Government has FAILED in every "government service" they have shoved down our throats while overspending our tax dollars.

Now, let's see,—*you* want to trust *these* folks with your plans for your retirement through tax-qualified plans!!?? Who has the problem here?

And, *you* look to *these* folks to educate your children? Amazing! **It must be because of the way you think!**

6

LIES, LIES, LIES!!

L ately, it has weighed heavily on my mind how dangerous it is to build your life on lies. It will never work! And the longer you let the lies prevail the worse the situation becomes. You can get to the point where you can't even identify a lie! That phenomenon is rampant in America.

Several months ago while I was riding down the Interstate Highway a semi-trailer truck passed me, and then transitioned over to the right hand lane in front of me. We rode along in tandem for a number of miles. On the back of the trailer was a sign that read, "This truck paid $8,423.00 in taxes last year." After a while it finally dawned on me that *this is a lie!* That truck didn't pay any taxes, nor did the company that owned it. The company's *customers* paid $8,423.00 in taxes last year for the freight that it hauled for them. The company was simply performing the function of *tax collector* in the form of higher freight rates than if the tax had not been imposed. Please don't try to tell me that it would just result in "windfall profits for the trucking company!" Competition between trucking companies makes sure of that. If that were not so, then truckers would charge just any price that they wished. If you are in the trucking business, just try it and see.

The company got a tax deduction for the taxes that it collected in the form of higher freight rates—*but the consumer didn't get any such treatment.* All he got to do was pay higher prices for the goods that he wanted to consume. *The consumer is the one who pays all taxes*!

Back in the days when George Wallace was Governor of Alabama I remember him saying during a re-election speech, "I'm going to reduce the taxes on all you 'little folks' and I'm going to increase the taxes on all those big corporations!" Lies, lies, lies!! Corporations don't pay taxes—they collect taxes from their customers in the form of higher prices than the consumer would have to pay otherwise.

A number of years ago I was trying to explain to a client and his wife (she ran the office, the payroll, etc.) that Social Security is a huge fraud—that there is no such thing as "the employee pays half of the tax and the employer pays the other half."

The employee pays it all! Her response was, "Oh, no! We pay half of the tax always! This is all the result of that scalawag, FDR, when Social Security was first adopted in the late 1930s. As it was then being discussed, it was first proposed to be "noncontributory", i.e., the employer was to "pay it all." But, then the genius of FDR appeared and he said, "No, let's make it 'contributory'—the employer will pay only half and the employee will pay the other half. That way the employee will **think** it is his own money. Now, by God, let's see anyone try to wreck my plan of Social Security!" He locked their minds on that thought and the vast majority of people in the U. S. have never gotten over it. Furthermore, I really don't think they ever will. That's because of how the government has conditioned them to think!

As I have said many times in the past—when it comes to things economic (or financial) few people understand what the play is about (Shakespeare is reputed to say that "all the world is a stage and all the people are actors thereon"). But what is worse—they can't keep the characters in the play straight! It appears to me that this is because they have an incredible ability to swallow lies. And the primary means of perpetuating these lies is the thing called government schools. Most people refer to them as "public schools" but I call them by their proper name—*government schools*. If you have a hard time accepting that fact, just ask any teacher or administrator to show you their paycheck and see *on whose account* it is drawn. It is a government! Learn from them and you will begin to *think* like them. I can't think of a worse thing to do to a fellow human being than cripple his mind! We have crippled minds at every turn in America today.

Discussing this fact recently with a client that is in the contracting business, he had this to add to the understanding: "When a Municipality lets a contract on a project and then attempts to place a penalty on the contractor if he does not finish by, say 90 days, yet the contractor is pretty sure that it will take 120 days, then the contractor is simply going to add a 'fudge factor' to his bid to cover the additional cost." All contractors that are bidding on the same project (and who feel the same way about the time restrictions) do the same thing. Who pays the additional cost? The taxpayer of the Municipality, that's who!! The consumer always pays for everything. Always has. Always will.

As some of you know, I sell books. Nearly all of them are sold in other states. That means they must be shipped to people in those locations, and this means shipping costs. I *don't* pay shipping costs—I add them to the cost of the books. If that cost were not isolated in the invoice, then I would have to simply charge a higher price for the books. When I had the printer ship the books to me, they did not pay the shipping charges; I paid them (and passed the cost on to customers in the form of higher book prices than would be without them). By the way, in the last shipment the freight invoice included a "fuel surcharge."

I could sell my books for forty percent less than I charge, if it weren't for income taxes. In fact, occasionally, when I meet someone for the first time, they may get around to asking me, "What sort of work do you do?" Sometimes I tell them, "I'm an *unpaid* IRS Tax Collector."

Similarly, suppose that some "highly paid executive" is negotiating with a company for possible employment and has concluded that he can get by on $300,000 per year after taxes. He knows full well that he is going to have to negotiate for compensation of $500,000 per year in order to have $300,000 left over after taxes, the only thing that he can spend. The $200,000 tax money is coming from his employer who then passes this on to consumers in the form of higher prices for goods produced or services rendered. The consumer pays all taxes.

Now, let's turn to some popular radio talk show hosts, e.g. Rush Limbaugh, Neal Boortz, Michael Reagan, et al. I hear them talk about "*All the taxes* are being paid by the rich folks— the poor don't pay any taxes at all." Lies, lies, lies! The *customers* of the "rich guys" pay all the taxes in the form of higher prices than they would have to pay for products without the taxes imposed on the producer of goods. The price of the goods is simply passed on to the consumer.

Just how many ways does one have to demonstrate this fact before the typical American begins to understand truth and cut out all these silly games that are *nothing more than lies*? I'm afraid it will take at least a century—if it ever does take place!

CHAPTER

ANTICIPATING A WINDFALL

Sometime in life most everyone experiences a financial "windfall" of significant proportions. Remembering that "wealth has got to reside somewhere" and that dividend-paying whole life insurance is an ideal location for it, then one needs to *anticipate* such an event by preparing a place to "dump" the windfall.

For instance, several years ago a piece of real estate that I owned finally sold. It was raw land, the epitome of a frozen asset. So, in comes this significant sum of money. What did I do with it? I paid off policy loans on a policy that I had bought thirteen years earlier. This policy was issued with a rating of "Preferred Plus"—the best rating one can get. Eighteen months later I was uninsurable as a result of coronary quad-bypass surgery.

When I bought the policy, I did not do it for death benefit alone. I bought it to create a place where I could put money that I could borrow to pay off the banks that were charging me outrageous interest rates. This procedure is obeying all the principles of Economic Value Added—the concept taught by Stern-Stewart Consulting firm in New York.

As this policy built up significant cash values, I borrowed from them and paid off the bank loans. This created large policy loan balances and became a place where I could pay off the policy loan with the net proceeds of the sale of the real estate. What if I had died during this period? The policy loan would have been paid off with the death benefit and the excess amount would have been paid to my beneficiary.

The net result of the procedure is this: When I paid off the policy loan, the result was the same thing as buying a new policy that year and "back-dating" the policy 13 years at Preferred Plus rating. That is an enormous advantage.

When I shared this story with fellow life insurance agents at that time, their response was, "You could have just bought Term Life Insurance at Preferred Plus rating—that would have been convertible to Whole Life Insurance—and you could have just paid off the banks directly."

Yes, that is true—*but I would have given up thirteen years of earning on the policy!*

Somehow or another that fact went right over their heads! It all has to do with *how a person thinks!* And the failure to recognize that the earlier a person starts a life policy—and the longer it is in force—the more efficient it becomes.

With this understanding established, consider this scenario: You and your spouse have a six-year old daughter. Sixteen years from now you are *going to have a financial windfall!* She is going to be 22 years old—and *hopefully,* she is going to be out of your household. And *hopefully,* she is not going to be a "boomerang kid" (they come back home—with another generation).

Maybe you have noticed that the cost of a child gets more and more expensive with age. It has become extremely expensive those last four years in this scenario. You have become accustomed to this outlay. Now she is out of your household—that expense is gone! That is a *financial windfall!*

If you don't have a place to put that windfall money, two things can happen—and both of them are bad. First of all, Parkinson's Law (see my previous book, *Becoming Your Own Banker*) will eat you alive! You will find "necessities" that you have just *got to have now,* but, somehow or another you managed to get along without them before!

Second possibility, you decide to create a place to warehouse this "newfound wealth" and you choose the best place to put it, i.e., a life insurance policy with a mutual dividend-paying company. You have got to start the policy at this point in time. There is no way of putting a significant lump sum into a new policy without it being classified as a Modified Endowment Contract.

The real penalty of delaying getting a policy started is the huge difference in cash value when one elects to get income at "passive income" time (that's my substitute for the word, "retirement"—a word that should never have come up).

The earlier one starts a life insurance policy, and the longer it stays in force, the more efficient it gets.

So, why not start up a new policy *now* and pay the annual premium for three of four years. Now, you can borrow from this new policy to pay the premiums due on it for the next *fourteen years!* This will create a place to put windfall money.

Now, let's consider the other end of life's spectrum. My Mother-in-law died a little over four years ago. She was in skilled nursing for three years—she was never coming home. It was only costing us $5,000 per month for this upkeep. When she died, that expense disappeared. We had a $60,000 per year windfall! We had a place to put that money—outstanding policy loans.

Nevertheless, Parkinson's Law manifested itself significantly. All kinds of items showed up that "we just had to have now," that we got along very well before this windfall! These were "necessities!" We are pretty good at battling that monstrous law, but it still was costing us an average of $1,500 per month.

I have been associated with the life insurance business for over 47 years and I have never heard anyone bring up this very valid point. I wonder why. Maybe it is because of the way people *think!*

CHAPTER

8

COMPREHENSIVE AND COLLISION
INSURANCE ON AUTOMOBILES

All forms of insurance are based on the probability of
loss of something during a time frame and correlating
that with the value thereof. Take the example of an accident
in an automobile. There are two things to consider in this
situation: (1) damage to some other person's life or property—
that is called Liability Insurance—and (2) damage to one's
own automobile—that is called Comprehensive & Collision
Insurance. C & C Insurance is required by the lender if one is
using a lender to make the auto purchase.

In the case of C & C coverage—the Insured pays a premium to an Automobile Insurance company to protect him in
case of something major happening, such as a total loss from a
wreck. The company pays the Insured from its pool of reserves,
less a deductible amount declared in the contract. In essence,
the Insured is simply "renting" that value from the Insurance
Company during the specified time frame.

This is all because most folks don't have a pool of reserves
of their own for such contingencies. Once a person has lots
of cash values in Dividend-paying Whole Life Insurance
and could sustain a total loss of an automobile without sig-

nificantly changing his lifestyle, then why not self-insure for Comprehensive and Collision coverage?

To illustrate, I have not bought C & C coverage for 34 years. Up to that time my total claims to the insurance company was only $1,500. Add up the premiums that I had paid from 1954 until 1980 and I could probably have bought a reasonable car. The auto insurance company "made out like a bandit" on me, didn't they?

So, I stopped insuring for C & C coverage and took the amount I was paying for it and added it to the next life insurance policy that I bought. Now, I'm self-insuring for C & C coverage. I'm making what the auto insurance company was making, tax-free.

Birmingham, AL is a hilly place, and from time to time we have ice storms in the winter. No one here knows how to drive a car under these conditions, including yours truly. Several years ago, like a fool, I was driving on the expressway in that type of weather and that truck in front of me stopped about 2 ½ inches faster than I did. Didn't do his bumper any harm but I "bent some sheet metal" out front of my car.

When I took it to the body shop the shop owner's first question, "Who is your insurance company?" My reply, "Sir, I don't have any C & C coverage." Do you know that there are "two prices"—one for those who are insured and one for those who are not? Guess which one is lower.

There are a number of other such things that can be avoided costs in life if you have a significant pool of cash value. But, be honest, for each of those things eliminated, you should add that same amount, or more, to another life insurance policy. There is no such thing as paying too much life premiums.

9

MY THOUGHTS ON UNIVERSAL LIFE, VARIABLE LIFE AND EQUITY INDEXED UNIVERSAL LIFE

U niversal Life was invented in the early 1980s by E. F. Hutton, a stock brokerage firm that, in my opinion, knew nothing about life insurance.

Remember the television commercial, "When E. F. Hutton speaks, everyone listens."

Have you heard him say anything lately? They don't exist anymore! UL was nothing more than "one-year term insurance with a side fund of an interest-bearing account." It was an attempt to "un-bundle" the savings element and the life insurance element of a whole life policy—something that can't be done, if one understands the concept of whole life insurance.

This happened during a time of high interest rates and it "looked good" in the early years of the policy. When I first saw the policy I ran some illustrations and they kept "falling apart" when the insured attained age 65 to 70. The cost of one-year term became prohibitive at the advanced ages and "ate up the cash fund" from that point forward. Therefore, I never sold one of them when I was in the business—and I surely wouldn't buy one!

Executive Life out in California bought the residue of E. F. Hutton. They made a "big splash" in the business and ultimately went broke. I understand that policy owners actually lost money with their policies.

Does the name, Michael Milken, mean anything to you? He did prison time as a result of his financial shenanigans. Would you guess where he was selling all of those "junk bonds?" If you replied, "Executive Life," then go to the head of the class! Would you like your financial future in the hands of people like that? How was Milken able to sell people on buying the stuff he offered? Maybe it was the greed of the American public.

Next, there came Variable Life, invented by Equitable Life Assurance Society. It was nothing more than one-year term insurance with a side fund of a mutual fund. There are more mutual funds than there are stocks. No mutual fund is any better than its manager. The great preponderance of mutual fund managers had never seen a down-turn in the market until the recent one.

I suggest that you read *The Truth About Mutual Funds*. Then read *The Battle for the Soul of Capitalism* by John Bogle, the originator of The Vangard Fund. These two books are vital to the understanding of what goes on in that industry. Also read *Pirates of Manhattan* by Barry Dyke, plus his follow-up book *The Pirates of Manhattan, II—Highway to Serfdom*. Upon completion of these four books you should be adequately informed to make an intelligent decision as to whether you should consider Variable Life.

I was with Equitable Life when Variable Life came on the scene. I never sold one of those policies—and I would never buy one. I do not recommend its use for the Infinite Banking Concept.

The tragedy of our times is that the life companies never spent any time on understanding Dividend-paying Whole Life Insurance and teaching the buying public its characteristics.

AND FINALLY, along comes the latest "new life insurance product"—Equity Indexed Universal Life—another attempt at "building a better mousetrap." I can think of no better expose of its fallacies than that presented by Todd Langford of Truth Concepts in Mt. Enterprise, TX. Full credit for this section of this book is given to him for his research and insight. Here is what he says about the subject:

The Top 10 Reasons NOT to BUY Equity Indexed Universal Life

By Todd Langford, www.truthconcepts.com Mt. Enterprise, Texas

Insurance companies have put numerous pages on the front of Equity Indexed Universal Life (EIUL) illustrations that describe the issues below, but most people (by design) will not take the time to read and understand what these pages are saying. I would encourage you to read those pages thoroughly before depending on an EIUL policy to increase your assets or protect your family. Similarly, Universal Life (UL) and its cousin Variable Universal Life (VUL) have some of the same problems so I've spelled out the issues below and placed an * next to the ones that are specific only to EIUL. As stated earlier, all Universal Life policies are a side fund (money market for regular UL, mutual fund-like separate accounts for VUL, and index fund-like accounts for EIUL) plus annually renewable, or one year increasing premium term insurance for the death benefit.

#10 Internal costs are not guaranteed

#9 Mortality charges are not guaranteed

#8 Market drops cause double pain

#7 Late premiums kill any guarantees

#6 Dividends from the index don't get credited*

#5 Participation ratios are often less than 100%*

#4 Returns are usually capped at various interest rates*

#3 Guarantees are not calculated annually*

#2 All of the above can be changed by the company

#1 The risk is shifted back to the insured

Now, let's look at each of these individually and tell the whole truth about the matter.

10. Internal administration fees charged against cash value on any type of Universal Life policy and shown on illustrations are run under current expense levels but those can change at the discretion of the company. Since the insurance company uses this money to run its operations, as prices of office supplies and real estate go up, they may choose to adjust these internal costs after you have bought the policy.

9. Mortality charges, what the insurance company charges for the death benefit are removed from the cash value or paid by premiums. In UL, these pay for annually increasing term insurance costs. This is true for any type of UL, no matter what the side fund is invested in. The cost for this one year term insurance can be changed at any time.

8. Market drops affect the side fund negatively no matter what the side fund is invested in. Since the death benefit is comprised of the One Year (or annually increasing) Term Insurance plus the side fund, any market drop causes double pain. Markets can drop regardless of whether they are supported by stocks or money markets. When the side fund is

reduced by a drop in the market or current interest rates, it now has less value so more Term Insurance must be bought to make up the difference which further reduces the side fund. Consequently you have double pain; less cash value and higher costs.

7. Any late premiums remove any guarantees in the policy. In most UL policies, even if the premium is finally paid, once it is late, the insurance company is off the hook for supporting any guaranteed premiums, cash value amounts or death benefits. In many cases, the insured may not even know that a premium was late and that the guarantees have been forfeited. Thinking about the time frame of a 50 year policy paid monthly (600 payments) ask yourself what the likelihood is of a mistake being made by the premium payer, their bank, the post office, the insurance company clerks or anyone else along the way?

*6. Equity Indexed Universal Life policies provide the policy holder no credit for any dividends from the stocks making up the index. The side fund of an EIUL isn't actually invested in the index; instead the index is used to determine the gross crediting rate for the side fund. If money were actually invested in the index, the investor would get both the change in Net Asset Value (whether up or down) AND the dividend income. However, in the case of EIUL, only the change in value of the index is the determining factor and the dividend is left out of the calculation entirely.

*5. Participation ratios are often less than 100%. As mentioned directly above, the side fund is not invested directly in the index and many insurance companies only credit a certain percentage of the increase in the market. Known as the participation ratio, this is often reported at 80% or less meaning you are getting only 80% of the increase in the market.

*4. Capping returns in order to keep high returns in the market from crediting too much to the side fund is a strategy many insurance companies use. The maximum return they'll give credit for may be at a certain percentage rate even though the index may have generated a higher percentage rate.

*3.Guaranteed minimum returns are not always calculated annually. Most EIUL policies have a guaranteed minimum return so that if the index drops below this rate, the insurance company will still credit at the guaranteed minimum rate. However, with some policies this guarantee is not applied annually but instead over an "indexing period" which could be 5–10 years. So you could have negative years in the index (below the guaranteed minimum rate) which would be applied to the side fund. This would cause a further reduction of value in excess of the guaranteed minimum rate in one particular year and as long as the overall average rate for the entire indexing period is not less than the guaranteed minimum rate, this would still count as meeting the minimum.

For example, if the minimum guaranteed rate is 2% inside a 5 year indexing period, you could have crediting rates of +13, –10, +10, –8 and +9% which would validate the promised guarantee because it would average more than 2% per year over the 5 years. The implication is that you cannot have a negative return, but as shown in the example below, you can have a negative return as long the guarantee is not calculated annually.

You'll notice another example below of the same interest rates, but with $100,000 of existing value instead of $10,000 per year of cash flow into the account.

2. At the discretion of the company any of the above factors can be changed at any time for the benefit of the company even after the policy has started. This is really one of the scari-

Cash Flow

Years:	5	
Present Value:		
Earning Rate:		

AVERAGE Investment Yield: 2.80%

ACTUAL Investment Yield: 2.01%

Year	Beginning of Year Acct. Value	Earnings Rate	Annual Cash Flow	Interest Earnings	End of Year Acct. Value
1		13.00%	10,000	1,300	11,300
2	11,300	(10.00%)	10,000	(2,130)	19,170
3	19,170	10.00%	10,000	2,917	32,087
4	32,087	(8.00%)	10,000	(3,367)	38,720
5	38,720	9.00%	10,000	4,385	53,105
Total	38,720	2.80%	50,000	3,105	53,105

Cash Flow

Years:	5	
Present Value:	100,000	
Earning Rate:		

AVERAGE Investment Yield: 2.80%

ACTUAL Investment Yield: 2.01%

Year	Beginning of Year Acct. Value	Earnings Rate	Annual Cash Flow	Interest Earnings	End of Year Acct. Value
1	100,000	13.00%		13,000	113,000
2	113,000	(10.00%)		(11,300)	101,700
3	101,700	10.00%		10,170	111,870
4	111,870	(8.00%)		(8,950)	102,920
5	102,920	9.00%		9,263	112,183
Total	102,920	2.80%		12,183	112,183

est aspects of all types of UL. There is no way to calculate what the outcome might be. Even if you analyzed the policy under the current structure and found it to be a viable tool, future changes could cause future problems.

1. Whereas, typically the point of all insurance purchased is to shift the risk from the insured to the company, all types of UL shift the risk backwards or from the insurance company to the insured.

With a mutual life insurance company, a whole life policy gives you a share of the entire profits of the company via dividends. The carrot being sold with EIUL is that it might exceed the return of a whole life policy. Yet this begs the question: How could the insurance company pay out more than the profits of the company and still be in business?

It has been explained to me that the insurance company buys options in the market to cover the risk of potentially having to credit any portion of high market returns in the index that exceeded their general portfolio rate to policy holder cash values. If this was a sound investment strategy, why wouldn't the insurance company use this strategy on their overall portfolio? I think the insurance company knows that the stock market is going to underperform their portfolio rate over time. This could reduce EIUL profits and increase the profits of the company, which then get distributed as dividends to whole life policy owners.

As a whole life policy owner, I should be pleased that EIUL could contribute additional profits to the company which might increase dividends to Whole Life, my concern is that EIUL policies are going to create a detrimental effect on the life insurance industry as a whole. I believe this may be the next major blight on the industry since under-funded Universal Life (UL) so heavily promoted in the 1980's. The unfortunate outcome is that any negative media affects the entire industry because the media doesn't differentiate between the new faulty products and the old tried and true whole life products that have been around for close to 200 years. As we know, the biggest danger with negative press is that is causes panic and the people will think the entire life insurance industry is bad and many perfectly structured whole life policies could get cancelled to the detriment of the policy holder and their family, just like what happened in the 1980's.

Remember #2 above, since the insurance company has the ability to change #10–3, they can always keep the Universal Life policies from outperforming their portfolio. Why would I want to take the safe portion of my assets and the protection of my family and expose it to risk? Doesn't that defeat the whole purpose of insurance? In my mind, I buy insurance and shift the risk to the insurance company, because they are experts at mitigating that risk and storing the cash to support it.

If you are seriously considering purchasing an EIUL product, please make sure you read and understand all the risks you and your family are assuming. Because of the complexity and numerous moving parts for this product, many of the people selling it that I've spoken with don't even understand it themselves. For me, I prefer a number of simple, guaranteed, tried and true whole life policies. These protect my Human Life Value and store my cash in the most efficient manner I know. Of course, the phenomenon we are addressing here is really nothing new to the world. St. Paul, in his epistle to Timothy warned him about it thousands of years ago.

> "Before God and Christ Jesus, who is going to
> judge the living and the dead, and by His appearing
> and His kingdom, I solemnly charge you: *proclaim*

the message [emphasis added]; persist in it whether convenient or not; rebuke, correct, and encourage with great patience and teaching. The time will come when **they will not tolerate sound doctrine, but according to their desires, will accumulate teachers for themselves because they have an itch to hear** *something new.* **They will turn away from hearing the truth and will turn aside to myths. [emphasis added]"**

—II TIMOTHY 4:1–4

What has been will be again, what has been done will be done again; there is nothing new under the sun.

—ECCLESIASTES 1:9

So, learn to live with it. That's the "ways of the world" and they have never been right about anything. All because of the way they **thought!**

How can you defend yourself against such nonsense? Learn from such people as Todd Langford, above—how he shows you exactly what is happening. If you know what's happening, you will know what to do.

10

ANNUITIES

What is an annuity? It is a contract between the owner and an insurance company. In return for payment made, the insurance company agrees to provide either a regular stream of income or a lump sum pay-out at some future time. Basically, it is the *reverse* of life insurance. It is taking a sum of money that has been accumulated and dissipating it over a certain period of time. This is hardly a place to warehouse your wealth! Why would one want to destroy wealth?

One type of annuity is nothing more than an accumulation account that turns into an annuity at a given time or age of the owner. Yet it is packaged and sold as "an annuity."

Another type is when an owner takes a lump sum that has been accumulated elsewhere and puts it into an *immediate annuity*, and thus begins to receive income right away in the form of principal and interest. Here, again, dissipating the accumulated wealth to zero over a period of time.

Suppose that an unexpected need for cash arises. Try borrowing from your annuity balance and see what happens! Of course, you could go to someone like J.G. Wentworth and put your annuity contract up as collateral. Check it out and see what that would cost you.

Contrast this thought process with all the illustrations that I show in my first book, *Becoming Your Own Banker*. Every one of them shows annual income from the policies and the ultimate death benefit doesn't disappear! The income received recaptures everything that was paid into the life policy in four to six years. And all this income can be tax free. That same income can be obtained by making policy loans, also tax-free. That is not so with an annuity.

For additional information on this point, please go back and study Chapter Two in this book. Notice that I have recovered everything I paid into the policy in only four years. That income was tax-free. Notice that I changed the dividend election to buying paid-up insurance after the four years, regardless of my insurability. Notice that I can now make a loan (each year) of the amount of the last check I received and that is not a taxable event. This will result in an ever-increasing loan against the values in the policy, but the death benefit is increasing faster than the increasing loan, resulting in a net death benefit that doesn't diminish. *If* people really understood the power of dividend-paying whole life insurance, they would never buy an annuity. I wonder why they do that. Probably because that's the way they **think!**

However, there can be a place where an *immediate annuity* could be good strategy. Suppose one had accumulated a significant sum of money elsewhere and would like to put it into life insurance. Basically, it can't be done. But, one could put that lump sum into an immediate annuity and use the income to buy life insurance, the perfect warehouse of wealth.

For more thoughts on this, go back and study Chapter Seven.

11

WHAT ABOUT PRECIOUS METALS?

At the time of this writing there are thousands of media commercials and newsletter articles warning of impending hyperinflation like the German experience in the 1920s. In contrast, Ben Bernanke is scared that we are going to have deflation so he wants to increase money supply (inflate) to prevent that possibility. Those who want to protect themselves from hyperinflation favor investing in gold and other precious metals.

·So, I ask a proponent of this persuasion, "If I am going to take your advice and buy gold, don't I have to buy it from someone who already owns the gold?" He replies affirmatively. "What does he want in exchange for his precious gold, I ask?" I find out that he wants my "worthless dollars!"

Why does he want to give up his precious Gold in exchange for my worthless dollars? If Gold is so valuable, why doesn't he just keep his gold? I still haven't had a response that makes sense.

While we are at conjecture, let's suppose that hyper-inflation does come about—and what if I buy gold bullion, as some advocates recommend. And what if my automobile

needs some repairs during this time—and what if the cost is
$749.00. Am I going to be able to take one of my gold bars
down to the repair shop and shave off enough gold to pay for
their service? I don't think so! Of course one could sell some
gold bullion for dollars and thus complete the automotive
repair transaction, but that involves going through a dealer of
some kind. That dealer will charge for this service. At the time
of this writing, the dealer on a prominent website will sell gold
bars for $1,723 per oz. If you want to sell it back to them, they
will pay you $1,593 per oz (plus shipping charges both ways).

So, silver coins made more sense to me. I might be able to
take a silver dollar and give it to the auto repair shop for an oil
change. I might take two or three and give to Jos.A.Bank in
exchange for a new suit.

Back in 1977 two associates and I bought some timberland in Alabama on Interstate 20. On part of this land there is
a prominent hill that is the highest point in that valley. About
22 years ago a cell-phone company approached us and wanted
to build a tower on that hill and lease the site from us for
five years with renewals each five years, the lease payments
increasing 20% each time.

The lease payments were deposited to my checking account
on April 1 each year. Last year the deposit to my account
was $2,075.00. Another couple of months go by and we are
approached by another firm that wanted to buy up our lease
in exchange for a lump sum. Since we are "senior citizens" we
thought this was an acceptable thing to do.

My share amounted to $15,000. Where should I "ware-
house" this windfall? Why not in silver, the radio commercial
suggested? Well, I knew the IRS was going to confiscate one-
third of the sum, so I had $10,000 to put into silver one ounce
Eagles—$44.00 each in June of 2011.

At lunch time yesterday, my wife comes into my office with the information from the radio commercial that "silver is up. . . ." So, I looked at the website of the firm where I bought my Silver Eagles. They will buy them back for $31.15 today and of course, I will have to pay the shipping cost! These commercials lie, don't they?

And, another thing—it is early April, 2012 at this time—if I still had that tower lease instead of the Silver Eagles, I would have $2,075.00 deposited to my checking account this week. I'm not going to tell you where I have those coins hidden, but I went to my secret hiding place to see if there was an additional $2,075.00 deposited there. Couldn't find any increase!

If I still had the tower lease, I would have another check for $2,075.00 next year also, wouldn't I? Etc. etc. etc.

But the media commercials and the newsletter writers said that investment in precious metals is the thing to do. What do you think?

Since I'm at my computer terminal, I checked the cash values of my life insurance policies and they had all gone up yesterday, they went up today and they will go up tomorrow.

Furthermore, did the German hyperinflation last forever? No, some sanity prevailed. There was a reversal. It did come to an end. Life goes on no matter what. Of course, it was a very painful experience that led to more nonsensical wars, but it was the natural result of the source of inflation—BANKERS!

Bankers lend money that doesn't exist. That is fraud! Therefore, if you have a bank loan of any kind, then you are part of the problem. Why would one want to "warehouse their wealth" with those folks when it can be done by contracting with like-minded people who cannot inflate. It is called Dividend-paying Whole Life Insurance with a Mutual Company.

12

OUT OF EGYPT, AND ON TO BABYLON—
FROM SLAVERY BACK TO SLAVERY

History seems to prove that mankind refuses to learn very much from extremely valuable experiences. I can think of no better place to prove my point than looking at the Bible. Mankind has an eternal problem—we want to be God (in the pagan sense of the word). To witness the ultimate manifestation of this malady, watch what we try to do with our government. Let's begin by going back several thousand years in the book of Genesis and start with:

GOD'S CONTRACT WITH JACOB (ISRAEL)

"I am the Lord, the God of your father Abraham and Isaac. I will give you and your descendants the land on which you are lying. Your descendants will be like the dust of the earth, and you will spread out to the west and to the east, to the north and to the south. All peoples on earth will be blessed through you and your offspring. I am with you and will watch over you wherever you go, and I will bring you back to this land. I will not leave you until I have done what I have promised you." (Genesis 28:13–15)

Jacob had a twin brother, Esau. In that day in time the firstborn received the birthright from the father. Esau was the older one. Jacob and his mother, Rebekah, through some trickery, managed to secure the birthright of the firstborn from his father, Isaac. Jacob was the favorite son of Rebekah. Esau was the favorite of Isaac. Naturally, this embittered Esau towards his brother, Jacob. Rebekah tells Jacob, "Your brother Esau is consoling himself with the thought of killing you. Now then, my son, do what I say: Flee at once to my brother Laban in Haran." (Genesis 27:42b–43)

And so, Jacob went to work for his Uncle Laban, who turned out to be a bigger trickster than Jacob and his mother! Laban had two daughters, Leah and Rachel.

Jacob told Laban he would work for him for seven years in exchange for his daughter, Rachel. Laban tricked him by giving him his oldest daughter, Leah. Then he said, "Work for me seven more years and I will give you Rachel." Laban really knew how to create a good deal for himself.

But, don't feel sorry for Jacob. He found a way to "get even" with Laban a few years later. Go and search it out for yourself—see Genesis 30:25–43. Apparently Jacob learned very well from Laban the art of deception!

Jacob had four sons by Leah—by her maid servant, and—by Rachel's maid servant for a total of ten sons. He finally gets to marry Rachel and she produces two sons—Joseph and Benjamin—they are Jacob's favorites, naturally creating all the makings of a dysfunctional family. Joseph could easily be classified by his ten older brothers as "a spoiled brat." Joseph was also "a dreamer"—and this characteristic comes in handy later in his life.

Somewhere along the time line, Jacob's name was changed to Israel.

A situation presents itself that the ten brothers can get Joseph out of their lives—and nothing could be better—by selling him to a caravan of tradesmen on their way to Egypt.

JOSEPH IS SOLD INTO SLAVERY

There, Joseph is sold into slavery. Another sequence of events places him in prison. We won't go into the details of this event. Again—search this one out for yourself, too. It is interesting reading. (Genesis 39)

Joseph was a model prisoner and worked himself up to becoming a "trusty." (Here we enter the concept of government. Pharaoh was government). Pharaoh's chief cupbearer and his chief baker were thrown into prison as a result of offending the king and were assigned to Joseph for custody. Both the cupbearer and the baker had a dream and Joseph correctly interprets them—the cupbearer will be restored to his position in three days!

Joseph instructs him, "But when all goes well with you, remember me to Pharaoh and get me out of this prison, for I was forcibly carried off from the land of the Hebrews, and even here I have done nothing to deserve being put in a dungeon."

The king's baker didn't fare too well. Interpreting his dream, Joseph said, "Within three days Pharaoh will lift off your head and hang you on a tree. And the birds will eat away your flesh." And so it came to be." (Genesis 40:19)

Unfortunately, the chief cupbearer did not remember Joseph—he forgot him! Imagine that!

Two years later Pharaoh has a dream but none of his servants can interpret it. Finally, his cupbearer remembers the abilities of Joseph and recommends him to Pharaoh.

Joseph interprets Pharaohs' dream. "Seven years of great abundance are coming throughout the land of Egypt, but seven years of famine will follow them. Then all the abundance in Egypt will be forgotten and the famine will ravage the land." (Genesis 41:29–30)

Because of this unique ability Joseph becomes second in command in all of Egypt, a rather rapid rise to power from such a lowly estate of being a prisoner!

During the "seven years of plenty" Pharaoh confiscated 20% of all the produce of the land. There is no evidence that he paid for it.

During the "seven years of famine" he *sold back to them, that which he had stolen!* So much for a government program! We tend today to think this kind of chicanery is a modern phenomenon—but, you see, it has deep roots going back thousands of years.

The famine was widespread and Israel, back in Canaan, learned that there was grain in Egypt. So, he sent his ten eldest sons to buy grain.

This resulted in a faceoff with Joseph, the one they had sold into slavery! Of course, they didn't recognize him. They thought he was probably a slave somewhere—or, maybe even dead. Joseph put them through a rather tough inquisition, but, eventually reconciliation was achieved.

"When the news reached Pharaoh's palace that Joseph's brothers had come, Pharaoh and all his officials were pleased." Pharaoh said to Joseph, 'Tell your brothers, do this: load your animals and return to the land of Canaan, and bring your father and your families back to me. I will give you the *best of the land of Egypt* [italics added] and you can enjoy the fat of the land.' (Genesis 45:16–18) 'Never mind about your belongings, because the best of all Egypt will be yours.'" (Genesis 45:20)

To my knowledge, this was among the first records of a government handout! As a student of Austrian Economics it is evident to me that, if you ever start taking that sort of stuff—you *will* end up being a slave!! It does something to one's mind and makes one dependent on the grantor. There is a very strong element of dependency in the act of worship. You will end up worshiping that on which you are dependent. And, that's what government people want you to do—be dependent on them. They want to be objects of worship. They want you to think that your blessings in life come from them—not from God! This is job security for government officials!

My personal observation down through the years has been—whenever there is a government handout of any kind, normally intelligent people will abandon their productive efforts, go stand in line for their share of the dole—and watch each other starve to death!! This point is the central theme of this chapter and it will be reemphasized as the story progresses.

And, now comes the hard part—the famine was severe throughout the whole region. "Joseph collected all the money that was to be found in Egypt and Canaan in payment for the grain they were buying, and he brought it to Pharaoh's palace." (Genesis 47:14) Eventually, they ran out of money.

Then they mortgaged their cattle. When they ran out of cattle, they mortgaged themselves. They became slaves for 430 years. In that many years you can really become good at slavery! You can't think past that situation. "As a man thinketh in his heart so is he," (Proverbs 23:7)

After a lengthy time Joseph dies and, "Then a new king, who did not know about Joseph, came to power in Egypt."

(Exodus 1:8) Things got much worse for the Israelite nation. Nothing in all the Scriptures indicates that God intended for His chosen people to end up in Egypt as slaves forever. To me, it seems that He let this experience happen to teach them that they should be dependent on Him—not government of any kind! Don't ever sell your souls to government, or you will end up in slavery. This is a lesson that they needed to learn early in their existence as a nation.

MOSES

So, after 430 years of slavery, surely they have learned what slavery looks like. Finally God produces Moses, a leader who will take them out of the slavery of Egypt and teach them how to be free men. God creates a situation in which Moses is reared in Pharaoh's household and consequently receives the best education possible at that time. In due time Moses becomes aware that he is not an Egyptian—but is an Israelite.

Sometime later Moses witnesses an Egyptian beating a Hebrew, one of his own people. "Glancing this way and that and seeing no one, he killed the Egyptian and hid him in the sand." (Exodus 2:12) And, of course, there were a couple of Egyptians who *did* see Moses' murder. Pharaoh heard of this and tried to kill Moses—but Moses escaped and went to live in Midian. While there, he married. He is living in this land for some 40 years.

It was during this time that Moses was tending the flock of his father-in-law, Jethro, near Mount Horeb. This is where he witnessed a strange sight—a bush was on fire, but it did not burn up! God spoke to him through the burning bush and directed him to go back to Pharaoh and bring His people out of Egypt.

God tells Moses, "And I will make the Egyptians favorably disposed toward this people, so that when you leave you will not go empty-handed. Every woman is to ask her neighbor and any woman living in her house for articles of silver and gold and for clothing, which you will put on your sons and daughters. And so you will plunder the Egyptians." (Exodus 3:21–22) In this manner God provided all the basic tools of a monetary system.

This was by no means an easy task. Pharaoh gave them all sorts of grief while God sent plague after plague to encourage him to "let my people go." This all took place over a lengthy period. The final plague that did the trick was the one that killed the first born of every Egyptian family—including Pharaohs' son. "During the night Pharaoh summoned Moses and Aaron and said, 'Up! Leave my people, you and the Israelites! Go, worship the Lord as you have requested. Take your flocks and herds, as you have said, and go. And also bless me.'" Exodus (12:31–32)

THE EXODUS

As the Israelites were leaving and approaching the Red Sea, Pharaoh had a change of heart—"*what have I done? I have let the Israelites go and have lost their services!*" So, they mount up their chariots and horses and pursue Moses and his followers. As Pharaoh and his troops approached them, the Israelites were terrified. Their backs were to the Red Sea and Pharaoh's Army was closing in!

God says to Moses: "Why are you crying out to me? Tell the Israelites to move on. Raise your staff and stretch out your hand over the sea to divide the water so that the Israelites can go through the sea on dry ground. I will harden the hearts of the Egyptians so that they will go in after them. And I will gain glory through Pharaoh and all his army, through his chariots and his horsemen. The Egyptians will know that I am the Lord when I gain glory through Pharaoh, his chariots and his horsemen." (Exodus 14:15–18)

And so, Pharaoh and his army were drowned right before their eyes!! Whew! What a narrow escape! What a miracle! Just how many miracles had the Israelites witnessed so far?

Now they are free of Egypt! Free at last! Free at last! And, where had God put them? *Sinai!* There was nothing there to sustain life. Nothing! This is where God put them for the next 40 years to teach them to be *dependent* on Him. It would be impossible for them to claim sustenance from any other source. Their minds had to be cleansed from the idea of being a slave. They had to learn to be free people, indeed, and put their trust in God—not government. No government programs!! Remember, there is a very strong element of dependency in the act of worship—*you will worship that on which you are dependent.* All governments want you to be dependent on them—not God!

GOD PROVIDES

Right away He provided them with the greatest document of human liberty that has ever been—*The Ten Commandments.* Exodus, chapter 20 details the commandments and for the next four chapters there are more explanations that would help them to understand further meaning of them. This lengthy explanation was apparently necessary to cleanse their minds from the paradigm of being a slave. You have to learn to *think* differently.

In Exodus, chapter 25, Moses goes up Mt. Sinai to meet with God and receive the tablets on which the Commandments are inscribed. He is up there for 40 days and nights.

The Israelite Nation had been grumbling and complaining ever since they realized they were in a place where they were totally dependent on God. Six weeks after crossing the Red Sea on dry land the whole community grumbled against Moses and Aaron. The Israelites said to them, "If only we had died by the Lord's hand in Egypt! There we sat around pots of meat and ate all the food we wanted, but you have brought us out into this desert to starve this entire assembly to death." (Exodus 16:2–3).

Now that Moses had been gone for a lengthy period, they were really angry. "When the people saw that Moses was so long in coming down from the mountain, they gathered around Aaron and said, 'Come, make us gods who will go before us. As for this fellow Moses who brought us up out of Egypt, we don't know what has happened to him.'" (Exodus 32:1).

Aaron responded, "Take off the gold earrings that your wives, your sons and your daughters are wearing and bring them to me." (Exodus 32:2) (Remember the Golden Rule— Those who have the gold make the rules!) Aaron took what they gave him and made it into an idol cast in the shape of a calf, fashioning it with a tool. The next day they had a big party! "We are saved! We are going back to Egypt—hallelujah!"

And, now, Moses came down from the mountain "and saw the calf and the dancing, his anger burned and he threw the tablets [inscribed Ten Commandments] out of his hands, breaking them to pieces at the foot of the mountain." (Exodus 32:19)

God instructed Moses to "utterly destroy" those who had instigated this event. Three thousand were killed that day. Moses goes up the mountain again and receives a second set of tablets with the Ten Commandments inscribed on them.

In Exodus 34:14, God reiterates the major point of the commandments, "Do not worship any other god, for the Lord whose name is Jealous, is a jealous [italics added] God."

In spite of the miracles that God showed them throughout their journey, they complained continually and longed to "be back in Egypt" in slavery. In Numbers 11 beginning at verse 4 we read, "The rabble with them began to crave other food, and again the Israelites started wailing and said, 'If only we had some meat to eat! We remember the fish we ate in Egypt *at no cost* [italics added]—also the cucumbers, melons, leeks, onions and garlic. But now we have lost our appetite; we never see anything but this manna!'"

At this point God became so exasperated with them that He put them on an Atkins Diet!! In verse 18 God says, "Tell the people: Consecrate yourselves in preparation for tomorrow, when you will eat meat. The Lord heard you when you wailed, 'If only we had meat to eat! We were better off in Egypt!' Now the Lord will give you meat, and you will eat it. You will not eat it for just one day, or two days or five, ten or twenty days, but for a whole month—until it comes out of your nostrils and you loathe it—because you have rejected the Lord, who is among you, and have wailed before Him, saying, 'Why did we ever leave Egypt?'" (Numbers:18–20)

Time and again, the Israelites complained so much that God was ready to do away with them all—except a remnant that remained loyal to Him—and start all over. Moses pled with God to spare them. However, a large number did perish from time to time.

FORTY YEARS OF EDUCATION

And so, they wandered in this wilderness for forty years, learning how to be dependent on God for sustenance. Their clothing did not wear out—their sandals did not wear out—He fed them, but, on occasion He tested them with a water problem. "Now there was no water for the community, and the people gathered in opposition to Moses and Aaron. They quarreled with Moses and said, 'If only we had died when our brothers fell dead before the Lord! Why did you bring the Lord's community into this desert, that we and our livestock should die here? Why did you bring us up out of Egypt to this terrible place? It has no grain or figs, grapevines or pomegranates. And there is no water to drink.'" (Numbers 20:2–5)

In response, "Moses and Aaron went from the assembly to the entrance to the Tent of Meeting and fell facedown, and the glory of the Lord appeared to them. The Lord said to Moses, 'Take the staff, and you and your brother Aaron gather the assembly together. *Speak* [italics added] to that rock before their eyes and it will pour out its water. You will bring water out of the rock for the community so they and their livestock can drink.'" (Numbers 20:6–8)

"So Moses took the staff from the Lord's presence, just as he commanded him. [But Moses was pretty "ticked off" at them]. He and Aaron gathered the assembly together in front of the rock and Moses said to them, 'Listen, you rebels, must we [italics added] bring you water out of this rock?' Then Moses raised his arm and *struck the rock twice* [italics added] with his staff. Water gushed out, and the community and their livestock drank." (Numbers 20:9–11)

This action on the part of Moses gives them the appearance that it was *Moses' power and the use of force* that solved their need for water—not the word of God. That was a big mistake on the part of Moses. As a result, he was not allowed to go into the Promised Land. He was allowed to view it from a distance, but that was all.

"But the Lord said to Moses and Aaron, 'Because you did not trust in me enough to honor me as holy in the *sight of the Israelites,* [emphasis added] you will not bring this community into the land I give them.'" (Numbers 20:12)

After wandering in the wilderness for some time, they finally came to the Promised Land. Moses says, "Then I said to you, 'You have reached the hill country of the Amorites, which the Lord our God is giving us. See, the Lord your God has given you the land. Go up and take possession of it as the Lord, the God of your fathers, told you. Do not be afraid; do not be discouraged.'" (Deuteronomy 1:20)

Whereupon—of all things—they had a committee meeting!! "Then all of you came to me and said, 'Let us send men ahead to spy out the land for us and bring back a report about the route we are to take and the towns we will come to.' The idea seemed good to me; so I selected twelve of you, one man from each tribe. They left and went up into the hill country, and came to the Valley of Eshcol and explored it. Taking with them some of the fruit of the land, they brought it down to us and reported, 'It is a good land that the Lord our God is giving us.'" (Deuteronomy 1:22–25)

"But, you were unwilling to go up; you rebelled against the command of the Lord your God." (Deuteronomy 1:26) "They say, 'The people are stronger and taller than we are; the cities are large, with walls up to the sky. We even saw the Anakites there.'" Caleb and Joshua were among the 12 spies and said, "We should go up and take possession of the land, for we can certainly do it." But, they got out-voted, ten to two, by the other spies who told all the people, "The land we explored devours those living in it. All the people we saw there are of great size. We seemed like grasshoppers in our own eyes, and we looked the same to them."

THE GRADUATE COURSE—BACK TO THE WILDERNESS!

As a result of this rebellion God gave them "the graduate course" in learning to be dependent on Him—they are back to more years of wandering in the wilderness! Except for Joshua and Caleb, all the adults who came out of Egypt perished during this time. Only their children finally made it to the Promised Land.

Before going in, God gave them a large number of briefings on what they were expected to do and reassurances that he would be with them—as long as they kept their end of the covenant.

So, after the 40 years had passed they finally are ready to go into the land that God had promised them. Moses is speaking. "Then I said to you, 'Do not be terrified; do not be afraid of them. The Lord your God, who is going before you, will fight for you, as he did for you in Egypt, before your very eyes, and in the desert. There you saw how the Lord your God carried you, as a father carries his son, all the way you went until you reached this place.'" (Deuteronomy 1:29–31)

"On the plains of Moab by the Jordan across from Jericho the Lord said to Moses, 'Speak to the Israelites and say to them: "When you cross the Jordan into Canaan, drive out all the inhabitants of the land before you. Destroy all their carved images and their cast idols, and demolish all their high places. Take possession of the land and settle in it, for I have given you the land to possess.'"" (Numbers 33:50–53)

"'But if you do not drive out the inhabitants of the land, those you allow to remain will become barbs in your eyes and thorns in your sides. They will give you trouble in the land where you will live. And then *I will do to you what I plan to do to them* [italics added].'"

Moses gives further instructions to them—"and when the Lord your God has delivered them over to you and you have defeated them, then you must destroy them *totally* [italics added]. Make no treaty with them, and show them no mercy. Do not intermarry with them. Do not give your daughters to their sons or take their daughters for your sons, for they will turn your sons away from following me to serve other gods, and the Lord's anger will burn against you and will quickly destroy you. This is what you are to do to them: Break down their altars, smash their sacred stones, cut down their Asherah poles and burn their idols in the fire." (Deuteronomy 7:2–5)

REMEMBER THE SOURCE OF BLESSINGS

Moses continues. "When you have eaten and are satisfied, praise the Lord our God for the good land he has given you. Be careful that you do not forget Him, failing to observe his commands, his laws, and his decrees that I am giving you this day. Otherwise, when you eat and are satisfied, when you build fine houses and settle down, and when your herds and flocks grow large and your silver and gold increase and all you have is multiplied, then your heart will become proud and you will forget the Lord your God, who brought you out of Egypt, out of the land of slavery." (Deuteronomy 8:10–14) "You may say to yourself, '***My*** [italics added] power and the strength of ***my*** [italics added] hands have produced this wealth . . . and so confirms his covenant, which he swore to your forefathers, as it is today. If you ever forget the Lord your God and follow other gods and worship and bow down to them, I testify against you today that you will surely be destroyed.'" (Deuteronomy 8:17–19)

This is a classical example of "the arrival syndrome" that I described in my previous book, *Becoming Your Own Banker*. I can't think of anything more detrimental to people than this!

Moses further explains to them: "After the Lord your God has driven them out before you, do not say to yourself, 'The Lord has brought me here to take possession of this land because of my righteousness.' It is not because of your righteousness or your integrity that you are going in to take possession of their land; but on account of the *wickedness of these nations*, [italics added] the Lord your God will drive them out before you, to accomplish what we swore to your fathers, to Abraham, Isaac and Jacob. Understand, then, that it is not because of your righteousness that the Lord your God is giving you this good land to possess, for you are a stiff-necked people." (Deuteronomy 9:4–6)

Did they carry out God's instructions? Absolutely not! "But Manasseh *did not* [italics added] drive out the people of Beth Shan or Taanach or Dor or Ibleam or Megiddo and their surrounding settlements, for the Canaanites were determined to live in that land. When Israel became strong, they pressed the Canaanites into *forced labor* [italics added] but never drove them out completely. Nor did Ephraim drive out the Canaanites living in Gezer, but the Canaanites continued to live there among them. Neither did Zebulun drive out the Canaanites living in Kitron or Nahalol, who remained among them; but they did subject them to *forced labor* [italics added]. Nor did Asher drive out those living in Acco or Sidon or Ahlab or Aczib or Helbah or Aphek or Rehob, and because of this the people of Asher lived among the Canaanite inhabitants of the land. Neither did Naphtali drive out those living in Beth Shemesh or Beth Anath; but the Naphtalites too lived among the Canaanite inhabitants of the land, and those living in Beth Shemesh and Beth Anath became *forced laborers* [italics added] for them." (Judges 1:27–33)

There are more examples cited, but you get the picture. Instead of driving them out, they *made slaves of them.* Since they were slaves in Egypt, did they *think* "this is the way to live?" All the adults who left Egypt perished in the wilderness wandering. Maybe this is just the nature of man—enslave others to benefit my own desires. Looking down through history, this seems to be the case.

JUDGES—BUT, NO GOVERNMENT

And so, for a lengthy period they lived under a system of Judges—*there was no government!* Under such freedom a nation cannot help but prosper! And, when you prosper, you can count on it—others will do their best to steal from you. That was the first labor-saving device—theft—don't produce anything, just steal what others produce.

The people said to Samuel, "'You are old, and our sons do not walk in your ways; now *appoint a king* [emphasis added] to lead us, such as all the other nations have.' But, when they said, 'Give us a king to lead us,' this displeased Samuel; so he prayed to the Lord. And the Lord told him: 'Listen to all that the people are saying to you; it is not *you* they have rejected as their king, but *me* [emphasis added]. As they have done from the day I brought them up out of Egypt until this day, forsaking me and serving other gods, so they are doing to you. Now listen to them; but warn them solemnly and let them know what the king who will reign over them will do.' (1 Samuel 8:5–9).

Samuel told all the words of the Lord to the people who were asking for a king. He said, 'This is what the king who will reign over you will do: He will take your sons and make them serve with his chariots and horses, and they will run in front of his chariots. Some he will assign to be commanders of thousands and commanders of fifties, and others to plow his ground and reap his harvest, and still others to make weapons of war and equipment for his chariots. He will take your daughters to be perfumers and cooks and bakers. He will take the best of your fields and vineyards and olive groves and give them to his attendants. He will take a tenth of your grain and of your vintage and give it to his officials and attendants. Your menservants and maidservants and the best of your cattle and donkeys he will take for his own use. He will take a tenth of your flocks, and you yourselves will become his slaves. When that day comes, you will cry out for relief from the king you have chosen, and the Lord will not answer you in that day.'" (1 Samuel 8:10–18).

And so, Samuel told them in no uncertain terms what a king would do to them. "But the people refused to listen to Samuel. 'No!' they said, 'We want a king over us. *Then we will be like all the other nations,* [emphasis added] with a king to lead us and to go out before us and fight our battles.'

When Samuel heard all that the people said, he repeated it before the Lord. The Lord answered, 'Listen to them and give them a king.'" (1 Samuel 8:19–22).

AT LAST, THEY HAVE A KING!
(GOVERNMENT)

Finally, Saul, son of Kish was chosen. "Then they ran and brought him out, and as he stood among the people he was a head taller than any of the others. Samuel said to all the people, 'Do you see the man the Lord has chosen? There is no one like him among all the people.' Then the people shouted, 'Long live the king!'" (1 Samuel 10:23–24)

Saul was a very successful soldier—big, strong, handsome—all the leadership qualities to be a king. And, he was a good man—very humble and surprised that he was to become king. To be anointed king was the ultimate experience one could have.

However, when one is placed in such a position, it is pretty easy to get off track. He began to think he was in charge. Today, the favorite word to describe this phenomenon is *hubris*. Just one little sin can go a long, long way. Samuel had warned of this probability, but no one listened. Saul was visible, and God was not. Saul overstepped his authority and thus sealed his fate. Man has one eternal problem—he wants to be God. To see the ultimate manifestation of this malady, watch what he tries to do with government. Power corrupts—and absolute power corrupts absolutely. So Saul went from good—to bad—to very bad over a period of time. Imagine that!

Soon it became evident to the Israelites that they had made a *big mistake!*

"The people all said to Samuel, 'Pray to the Lord your God for your servants so that we will not die, for we have added to all our other sins the evil of asking for a king.'" (1 Samuel 12:19)

'Then the word of the Lord came to Samuel: 'I am grieved that I have made Saul King, because he has turned away from me and has not carried out my instructions.'" (1Samuel 15:10)

His successor was David, a man after God's own heart. Down through the ages, he was recognized as *the* great king of all time. But, David goofed up in a big way—his involvement with Bathsheba. David tried to "worm his way out of the situation," but Nathan, the prophet brought him face to face with the error of his ways. Do you realize what a brave man Nathan was? He could easily have had his head cut off for his action. (Sometimes I wonder—where is Nathan today? We need Nathan badly!) Unlike Saul, though, David repented. "Then David said to Nathan, 'I have sinned against the Lord.'" (2 Samuel 12:13)

But, no matter how "good" a person may be, he will still reap the consequences of that kind of action. It can manifest itself in any number of ways. In this case, one of the results was a totally dysfunctional family.

First, his son Amnon raped his half-sister, Tamar. Her brother by the same mother was Absalom. A couple of years later, Absalom found a way to kill Amnon because of what he had done to Tamar. Then he fled to another kingdom and stayed there three years. Finally King David was persuaded to let Absalom return to Jerusalem. "But the king said, 'He must go to his own house; he must not see my face.'" (2 Samuel 14:24)

"In all Israel there was not a man so highly praised for his handsome appearance as Absalom. From the top of his head to the sole of his foot there was no blemish in him." (2 Samuel 14:25)

Absalom lived two years in Jerusalem without seeing the king's face. Finally the two were reconciled and they met.

"In the course of time Absalom provided himself with a chariot and horses and with fifty men to run ahead of him. He would get up early and stand by the side of the road leading to the city gate. Whenever anyone came with a complaint to be placed before the king for a decision, Absalom would call out to him, 'What town are you from?'

He would answer, 'Your servant is from one of the tribes of Israel.' Then Absalom would say to him, 'Look, your claims are valid and proper, but there is no representative of the king to hear you.' And Absalom would add, 'If only I were appointed judge in the land! Then everyone who has a complaint or case could come to me and I would see that he gets justice.'

Also, whenever anyone approached him to bow down before him, Absalom would reach out his hand, take hold of him and kiss him. Absalom behaved in this way toward all the Israelites who came to the king asking for justice, and so he stole the hearts of the men of Israel." (2 Samuel 15:1–6) He would solve all of their problems if they would only come to him and ask!

So, you see, politicians have had a superior model to sway the hearts of men since ancient days. If Absalom were alive in America today, he would be elected President in a heartbeat! Continuing this kind of action for several years, now Absalom decided that he was to become king in place of his father, David, and set out to kill him. Nice guy, huh? This all ended in tragedy and the death of Absalom. King David was devastated in the loss of his errant son.

Continuing the saga: "Now, Adonijah, whose mother was Haggith, put himself forward and said, 'I will be king.' So he got chariots and horses ready, with fifty men to run ahead of him. (His father had never interfered with him by asking,

'Why do you behave as you do?' He was also very handsome and was born next after Absalom.)" (1 Kings 1:5–6) Adonijah proceeded to have parties and surrounded himself with dignitaries of his own choosing.

SOLOMON—WISEST MAN OF ALL TIME

This was not to be, however, and David's choice for his successor was Solomon, the son of David and Bathsheba. Needless to say, Adonijah ended up losing his life in this intrigue. In fact, there was a lot of killing that took place during all this scene of David's household.

Solomon started his reign with the best of intentions. In 1 Kings he says, "Now O Lord my God, you have made your servant king in place of my father David. But I am only a little child and do not know how to carry out my duties. Your servant is here among the people you have chosen, a great people, too numerous to count or number. So give your servant a discerning heart to govern your people and to distinguish between right and wrong. For who is able to govern this great people of yours?" (1 Kings 3:7–10)

In verses 11 and 12, "So God said to him, 'Since you have asked for this and not for long life or wealth for yourself, nor have asked for the death of your enemies but for justice, I will do what you have asked. I will give you a wise and discerning heart, so that there will never have been anyone like you, nor will there ever be.'" 1 Kings 3:11–12)

Solomon was the wisest man of all time. But, if the wisest man of all time could mess up as badly as he did, what hope do you and I have without God? How could Solomon be stupid enough to have 700 wives and 300 concubines? Just think of how many mothers-in-law goes with a situation like that! Also, many of those marriages were the result of alliances with other nations. History clearly shows the tragic results of such a course of action. At the very beginning of his reign Solomon made an alliance with Pharaoh King of Egypt and married his daughter.

As a side note, remember in the early years of our own country, George Washington, in his farewell address, warned against any entangling alliances with foreign nations. So did Jefferson and Madison. We seem to have forgotten their warnings and we are reaping the consequences now.

Then he proceeds to build this huge temple. "The temple that King Solomon built for the Lord was sixty cubits long, twenty wide and thirty high." (I Kings 6:2)

According to my Bible, that would be 90 feet long, 30 feet wide and 45 feet high. (I Kings 6:37 b)—Solomon spent *seven* years building the temple.

For a complete account of what went into the Temple and Solomon's palace I urge you to read 1 Kings Chapter 6 and 7.

Next, he builds his own palace "It took Solomon *thirteen years* [italics added], however to complete the construction of his palace." It was "a hundred cubits long, fifty wide and thirty high." (I Kings, 7:1–2) (150 feet long, 75 feet wide and 45 feet high). Note the comparison of the relative size and time that it took to build the two structures. Can you imagine the taxation required to build all this? I wonder why his palace was so much larger.

Additionally, it was all done with slave labor. In 1 Kings 9:15 we read, "Here is the account of the forced labor King Solomon conscripted to build the Lord's Temple, his own palace, the supporting terraces, the wall of Jerusalem, and Hazor, Megiddo, and Gezer." In verse 20–23, "All the people left from the Amorites, Hittites, Perizzites, Hivites and Jebusites (these peoples were not Israelites), that is, their descendants remaining in the land, whom the Israelites could not exterminate—these Solomon conscripted for his slave labor force, as it is to this day. But, Solomon did not make slaves of any of the Israelites; they were his fighting men, his government officials, his officers, his captains, and the commanders of his chariots and charioteers. They were also the chief officials in charge of Solomon's projects—550 officials supervising the men who did the work." (1 Kings 9:20–23) Bureaucracy never changes either, does it?

In addition to all this extravagance I suggest that you read 1 Kings 11 for a more complete description of the wealth he accumulated.

"When Solomon had finished building the temple of the Lord and the royal palace, and had achieved all he had desired to do, the Lord appeared to him a second time, as he had appeared to him at Gibeon. The Lord said to him: 'I have heard the prayer and plea you have made before me; I have consecrated this temple, which you have built, by putting my Name there forever. My eyes and my heart will always be there.'

'As for you, if you walk before me in integrity of heart and uprightness, as David your father did, and do all I command and observe my decrees and laws, I will establish your royal throne over Israel forever, as I promised David your father when I said, 'You shall never fail to have a man on the throne of Israel.'

'But if you or your sons turn away from me and do not observe the commands and decrees I have given you and go off to serve other gods and worship them, then I will cut off Israel from the land I have given them and will reject this

temple I have consecrated for my Name. Israel will then
become a byword and an object of ridicule among all peoples.
And though this temple is now imposing, all who pass by will
scoff and say, 'Why has the Lord done such a thing to this
land and to this temple?'

People will answer, 'Because they have forsaken the Lord
their God, who brought their fathers out of Egypt, and have
embraced other gods, worshiping and serving them—this is
why the Lord brought all this disaster on them.'" (1 Kings
9:1–9)

But, in 1 Kings 11:1–6 we read: "King Solomon, however,
loved many foreign women besides Pharaoh's daughter—
Moabites, Ammonites, Edomites, Sidonians and Hittites.
They were from nations about which the Lord had told the
Israelites, 'You must not intermarry with them, because they
will surely turn your hearts after their gods.' Nevertheless,
Solomon held fast to them in love. He had seven hundred
wives of royal birth and three hundred concubines, and his
wives led him astray. As Solomon grew old, his wives turned
his heart after other gods and his heart was not fully devoted
to the Lord his God, as the heart of David his father had
been.

He followed Ashtoreth the goddess of the Sidonians, and
Molech the detestable god of the Ammonites. So Solomon
did evil in the eyes of the Lord; he did not follow the Lord
completely, as David his father had done." (1 Kings 11:1–6)

And in verses 9–13, "The Lord became angry with
Solomon because his heart had turned away from the Lord,
the God of Israel, who had appeared to him twice. Although
he had forbidden Solomon to follow other gods, Solomon did
not keep the Lord's command. So the Lord said to Solomon,
'Since this is your attitude and you have not kept my covenant

and my decrees, which I commanded you, I will most certainly tear the kingdom away from you and give it to one of your subordinates. Nevertheless, for the sake of David your father, I will not do it during your lifetime. I will tear it out of the hand of your son. Yet I will not tear the *whole* kingdom from him, but will give him one tribe for the sake of David my servant and for the sake of Jerusalem, which I have chosen.'" (1 Kings 11:9–13)

And so, Solomon sealed his fate. After his death, his son, Rehoboam, became king. "And the whole assembly of Israel went to Rehoboam and said to him: 'Your father put a heavy yoke [taxes] on us, but now lighten the harsh labor and the heavy yoke he put on us, and we will serve you.' Rehoboam answered, 'Go away for three days and then come back to me.' So the people went away. Then King Rehoboam consulted the elders who had served his father Solomon during his lifetime. 'How would you advise me to answer these people?' he asked. They replied, 'If today you will be a servant to these people and serve them and give them a favorable answer, they will always be your servants.'

But Rehoboam rejected the advice the elders gave him . . ." [He wanted *power* and consulted the young men who had grown up with him and were serving him.] "He asked them, 'What is your advice? How should we answer these people who say to me 'Lighten the yoke [reduce taxes] your father put on us'?'" (1 Kings 12:3 –9)

TAXES, TAXES, TAXES!

"The young men who had grown up with him replied, 'Tell these people "My little finger is thicker than my father's waist. My father laid on you a heavy yoke; I will make it even heavier.

My father scourged you with whips; I will scourge you with scorpions.'" (1 Kings 12:10–11)

So, this was the course of action by Rehoboam—even heavier taxation. Guess what? This results in the division of the kingdom. Ten tribes become the Northern Kingdom under the rule of Jereboam, who was one of Solomon's officials many years prior—thus fulfilling the promise God made earlier (three paragraphs above). Onerous taxation has been a primary factor in division of nations all throughout history. I'm sure it was so in this case, too.

In 1776 thirteen independent colonies seceded from the mother country, England, and went to war for ten years on account of outrageous taxation. It was two percent in the South and one percent in the North! As Charles Adams, the tax attorney says in his book, *For Good and For Evil,* "behind every significant event in history, there is a tax story."

"When all Israel saw that the king [Rehoboam] refused to listen to them [because of the outrageous taxation], they answered the king: 'What share do we have in David, what part in Jesse's son? To your tents, O Israel! Look after your own house, O David!' So the Israelites went home. But as for the Israelites who were living in the towns of Judah, Rehoboam still ruled over them. King Rehoboam sent out Adoniram, who was in charge of forced labor, but all Israel stoned him to death. King Rehoboam, however, managed to get into his chariot and escape to Jerusalem. So Israel has been in rebellion against the house of David to this day." (1 Kings 12:16–19)

King Jeroboam had problems with his thought processes almost immediately. Because of his fear that the kingdom would be reunited, he took measures to lead the Northern Kingdom to worshiping idols.

"Go, tell Jeroboam that this is what the Lord, the God of Israel, says: 'I raised you up from among the people and made you a leader over my people Israel. I tore the kingdom away from the house of David and gave it to you, but you have not been like my servant, David, who kept my commands and followed me with all his heart, doing only what was right in my eyes. You have done more evil *than all who lived before you* [emphasis added]. You have made for yourself other gods, idols made of metal; you have provoked me to anger and thrust me behind your back. Because of this, I am going to bring disaster on the house of Jeroboam. I will cut off from Jereboam every last male in Israel—slave or free. I will burn up the house of Jeroboam as one burns dung, until it is all gone.'" (1 Kings 14:7–11)

So, Jeroboam's kingdom only lasted 22 years. Judah, under King Rehoboam was no better—they did evil in the sight of the Lord—and his kingdom only lasted 17 years. There was continual warfare between the two kingdoms during their reigns.

Thereafter, there was a succession of kings and a continuous downward spiral of evil. Every once in a while there was a good guy, like Hezekiah and Josiah, but, generally speaking it was not a very pretty picture that followed for many years. All the things that Samuel had warned them about when they asked for a king had now taken place. But, search the scriptures diligently and you will find no place where they lamented asking for a king except the occasion just after King Saul when they recognized their mistake.

BACK IN SLAVERY

As a result of all the sins of the Northern Kingdom they were first to be taken into exile by a foreign nation. "The king of

Assyria invaded the entire land, marched against Samaria and laid siege to it for three years. In the ninth year of Hoshea, the king of Assyria captured Samaria and deported the Israelites to Assyria." (2 Kings 17:5–6)

A number of year's later Judah fell to the same fate as a result of their sins. They were taken to *Babylon and their city of Jerusalem and the temple was reduced to rubble. Now they were all* back in the slavery they had experienced in Egypt. They had rejected their dependence on God and had adopted the ways of all the other nations.

All of this explanation has been to bring the story to the book of Ezekiel. The Southern Kingdom is in exile and in Chapter 23 Ezekiel is revealing to them the message from God telling them how they came to this fate. When one ends up in an awful mess, one needs to understand "how you got here."

If this fact is not clear, then you are doomed to make the same mistakes over and over. This is the bane of man's existence.

GOD'S MESSAGE TO EZEKIEL

Following is the entire 23rd chapter:

> The word of the Lord came to me: "Son of man, there were two women, daughters of the same mother. *They became prostitutes in Egypt* [italics added], engaging in prostitution from their youth. In that land their breasts were fondled and their virgin bosoms caressed. The older was named Oholah and her sister was Oholibah. They were mine and gave birth to sons and daughters. Oholah is Samaria, and Oholibah is Jerusalem.
>
> "Oholah engaged in prostitution while she was still mine; and she lusted after her lovers, the Assyrians—

warriors clothed in blue, governors and commanders, all of them handsome young men, and mounted horsemen. She gave herself as a prostitute to all the elite of the Assyrians and defiled herself with all the idols of everyone she lusted after. She did not give up the prostitution *she began in Egypt* [italics added], when during her youth men slept with her, caressed her virgin bosom and poured out their lust upon her.

"Therefore I handed her over to her lovers, the Assyrians, for whom she lusted. They stripped her naked, took away her sons and daughters and killed her with the sword. She became a byword among women, and punishment was inflicted on her.

"Her sister Oholibah saw this, yet in her lust and prostitution she was more depraved than her sister. She too lusted after the Assyrians—governors and commanders, warriors in full dress, mounted horsemen, all handsome young men. I saw that she too defiled herself; both of them went the same way.

"But she carried her prostitution *still further* [italics added]. She saw men portrayed on a wall, figures of Chaldeans portrayed in red, with belts around their waists and flowing turbans on their heads; all of them looked like Babylonian chariot officers, natives of Chaldea. As soon as she saw them, she lusted after them and sent messengers to them in Chaldea. Then the Babylonians came to her, to the bed of love, and in their lust they defiled her. After she had been defiled by them, she turned away from them in disgust. When she carried on her prostitution openly and exposed her nakedness, I turned away from her in disgust, just as I had turned away from her sister. Yet she became more and more promiscuous as recalled the days of her youth, *when she was a prostitute in Egypt* [italics added]. There she lusted after her lovers, whose genitals were like those of donkeys and whose emission was like that of horses. So you longed for the lewdness of your youth, *when in Egypt* [italics added] your bosom was caressed and your young breasts fondled.

"Therefore, Oholibah, this is what the Sovereign Lord says; I will stir up your lovers against you, those you turned away from in disgust, and I will bring them against you from every side—the Babylonians and all the Chaldeans, the men of Pekod and Shoa and Koa, and all the Assyrians with them, handsome young men, all of them governors and commanders, chariot officers and men of high rank, all mounted on horses. They will come against you with weapons, chariots and wagons and with a throng of people; they will take up positions against you on every side with large and small shields and with helmets. I will turn you over to them for punishment, and they will punish you according to their standards. I will direct my jealous anger against you, and they will deal with you in fury. They will cut off your noses and your ears, and those of you who are left will fall by the sword. They will take away your sons and daughters, and those of you who are left will be consumed by fire. They will also strip you of your clothes and take your fine jewelry. So I will put a stop to the lewdness and prostitution *you began in Egypt* [italics added]. You will not look on these things with longing or remember Egypt anymore.

"For this is what the Sovereign Lord says: I am about to hand you over to those you hate, to those you turned away from in disgust. They will deal with you in hatred and take away everything you have worked for. They will leave you naked and bare, and the shame of your prostitution will be exposed. Your lewdness and promiscuity have brought this upon you, *because you lusted after the nations and defiled yourself with their idols* [italics added]. You have gone the way of your sister; so I will put her cup into your hand.

"This is what the Sovereign Lord says; "You will drink your sister's cup, a cup large and deep; it will bring scorn and derision, for it holds so much. You will be filled with drunkenness and sorrow, the cup of ruin and desolation, the cup of your sister Samaria. You will drink it and drain it dry; you will dash it to pieces and tear your breasts. I have spoken, declares the Sovereign Lord.

"Therefore this is what the Sovereign Lord says; Since you have forgotten me and thrust me behind your back, you must bear the consequences of your lewdness and prostitution."

The Lord said to me; "Son of man, will you judge Oholah and Oholibah? Then confront them with their detestable practices, for they have committed adultery and blood is on their hands. They committed adultery with their idols; they even sacrifice their children, whom they bore to me, as food for them. They have also done this to me: At that same time they defiled my sanctuary and desecrated my Sabbaths. On the very day they sacrificed their children to their idols, they entered my sanctuary and desecrated it. That is what they did in my house.

"They even sent messengers for men who came from far away, and when they arrived you bathed yourself for them, painted your eyes and put on your jewelry. You sat on an elegant couch, with a table spread before it on which you had placed the incense and oil that belonged to me.

"The noise of a carefree crowd was around her; Sabeans were brought from the desert along with men from the rabble, and they put bracelets on the arms of the woman and her sister and beautiful crowns on their heads. Then I said about the one worn out by adultery, 'Now let them use her as a prostitute, for that is all she is.' And they slept with her. As men sleep with a prostitute, so they slept with those lewd women, Oholah and Oholibah. But righteous men will sentence them to punishment of women who commit adultery and shed blood, because they are adulterous and blood is on their hands.

"This is what the Sovereign Lord says: Bring a mob against them and give them over to terror and plunder. The mob will stone them and cut them down with their swords; they will kill their sons and daughters and burn down their houses.

"So I will put and end to lewdness in the land, that all women may take warning and not imitate you. You will suffer the penalty for your lewdness and bear the consequences of your sins of idolatry. Then you will know that I am the Sovereign God."

So, out of the slavery of Egypt—and back to slavery in Babylon. They put their dependence on earthly kings instead of God. It didn't work for them at that time and it won't work for us today.

CONCLUSION

When the Israelite nation left Egypt, God explained right away that HE was their king. They did not need an earthly king. They were to put their dependence in Him, not earthly leaders.

Again, mankind's eternal problem is that he wants to be god. To observe the ultimate manifestation of the malady, watch what he tries to do with his government.

God further explained that he was *a Jealous God*—He won't put up with that nonsense! As a result, mankind is always destined to fail in such attempts. There has never been a Socialist, Fascist, Communist, Statist, etc. society that has lasted very long. They are all doomed to failure because of this faulty premise.

But, as a result of his arrogance, mankind keeps doing the same stupid thing. Now that you see my thesis, you can translate Egypt, Babylon, Rome, and Washington DC! If you have seen one, you have seen them all!

Today, United States citizens are totally dependent on Washington! If you don't believe it, try to take away a government program of some kind. Americans cannot conceive of life without government programs. Yet, Christians claim that they worship God. Based on their behavior, I don't believe it. They are back in slavery and can't even recognize their situation.

SOLUTION

Turn back to God. Focus our relationships on Him. Worship the Almighty daily in all that we do; in our homes, our work, our friendships. Recognize that He is our sustainer, Creator, the "Alpha and Omega." Make a Joyful noise unto the Lord.

Serve the Lord with gladness. Know that it is He that has
made us and not we ourselves. Come before His presence
with Thanksgiving. Be thankful unto Him and bless His name
(Psalms 100). Change our mindset to Him. (Change the way
you *think*) This will take a lot of work and effort. It will change
us. Do you want to undergo this? It is a conscious decision.
God has given us the tools to do this. We have fallen woefully
short. It starts with me, it starts with you. It can spread. It is
God centered, God directed.

It will not start with government directed programs (i.e.
"Faith Based Initiatives," Social Security, War on Poverty,
Social Restructuring, Equal Opportunity, OSHA, rise of the
proletariat, Government/Business collaboration, Welfare,
Warfare, "My country right or wrong," Patriotism, Remember
Pearl Harbor, Remember the Maine, Remember 9/11, et al).

Our strongest position will be on our knees, seeking His
face, His will, and constantly seeking His guidance in all that
we do. This is a tremendous challenge, given our past performance. Thank God for His plan for our salvation, which
He outlined from the beginning. That plan was Jesus . . . not
democracy, not statism, not Kings, not fascism, not commu-
nism, not popery, not sharia. We struggle on like sheep with
our futile schemes of self government, ignoring the Way our
Father in Heaven has provided. When will we learn?

MORE THINGS TO PONDER IN
THIS BIBLICAL STORY

When the Israelites were "guests" in Egypt and the seven years
of famine came about, Pharaoh sold back to the people that
which he had confiscated! Pharaoh ended up with all the gold!
All governments have that characteristic.

Fast forward a bit and Moses has demonstrated that Pharaoh should let them leave Egypt. Now, look at Exodus 12:35–36. The Israelites did as Moses instructed and asked the Egyptians for articles of silver and gold and for clothing. The Lord had made the Egyptians favorably disposed toward the people, and they gave them what they asked for; so they *plundered the Egyptians*. [Italics are mine].

Do you think for one minute that they needed this silver and gold to buy things from the local Wal-Mart that they would find over in Sinai while on their way to their promised land? I don't think so! Maybe—just maybe—God saw that mankind needs some means of transacting business with one another no matter what the circumstances.

When they finally got into their new land, they naturally prospered. History seems to record this sort of thing when people don't have a King (government). But, their mindset couldn't conceive of life without a King. This produced a series of Kings over many years and led to King Solomon, "the wisest man of all time."

Check out I Kings chapter 10 and see the account of all the gold and silver and all sorts of other items of wealth that Solomon accumulated. Pray tell, how is it that governments, whatever form they may take, always end up with so much wealth? It is always taxation of some sort!

Solomon dies and his son, Rehoboam becomes his successor as King. His subjects are rebelling because of the heavy burden (taxes) that Solomon had imposed upon them. Rehoboam asks the advice of his senior advisors, "What to do?" They advised him to lighten up the burden but, like all

---

*All passages of the Bible cited in this book are taken from the New International Version.

government leaders down through history, he wanted power! So, he went to his peer advisors who told him to double the burden and show them what governing powers are really like.

This caused a division of the kingdom. The ten northern tribes seceded! In time to come there were a couple of kings in the southern kingdom that were good men, but a series of kings that followed in both nations followed "the ways of the world" and, as night follows the day, both kingdoms ended up back in slavery, captives of foreign nations!

And so, the Israelite nation started out becoming slaves of a foreign government, Pharaoh. They migrate to the land God promised them and got their own series of kings, who led them back to slavery in foreign lands!

Thirteen, independent British Colonies seceded from their mother country in 1776 on account of outrageous taxation. Do your own research of its level at that time. Internet search engines make that information readily available. In 1789, this confederation of independent states ratified a constitution and became the USA we know today. Now, research the level of taxation that we live under today. And we have politicians who tell us that this is *freedom!!*

We have two major political parties today. Distill their platforms to their essence and they amount to no more than "Our brand of coercion (slavery) is better than their brand of coercion (slavery)." Neither objects to coercion, only its level, which always tends to increase with time.

CONCLUSION

We have looked at a lot of valuable history in the previous chapter. Does mankind really ever learn very much? Apparently we don't. Technology changes the way we do things but our thought processes seem to make the same old mistakes. We look to government to solve all our problems—and they can't do it. They all have perfect records of failure. All that action is just "man trying to play god in the pagan sense of the word." God is a jealous God! He won't put up with that nonsense.

There is a tremendous element of dependency in the act of worship. You will worship that on which you are dependent. Americans today cannot visualize life without a government program of some sort. Absurd!

Why does one depend on a government program for his financial future? *Think about it!*

Read history and look how mankind has turned the "warehousing of wealth" function over to bankers. Look at how their activity is totally intertwined with government. They have plunged the entire world into the worst financial situation of all time. It doesn't have to be this way. The warehousing of wealth function should be held entirely at the "you and me" level. It can be—and is being done—by those who *think about it!*

There is one major caveat—beware of the *Human Factors* as I described in *Becoming Your Own Banker!* They are listed here in the same order as in *Becoming Your Own Banker:*

1. Parkinson's Law

2. Willie Sutton's Law

3. The Golden Rule

4. The Arrival Syndrome

5. Use It or Lose It

Start learning how you can change your life by attacking the following reading list and the recommended websites listed in this book.

A word of caution—this may change the way you *think!* Good luck!

RECOMMENDED READING LIST

Books that support *Building Your Warehouse of Wealth* ...

A Path to Financial Peace of Mind by Dwayne Burnell
Becoming Your Own Banker by R. Nelson Nash
EVA: The Real Key to Creating Wealth by Al Ehrbar
Family Wealth Counseling by E.G. 'Jay' Link
Fooled by Randomness by Nassim Nicholas Taleb
Foundations of Economic Value Added by James L. Grant
How Privatized Banking Really Works by L. Carlos Lara and
    Robert P. Murphy, Ph.D.
Life Insurance—Will It Pay When I Die? by Thomas Young
Prescription for Wealth by Dr. Tomas P. McFie

HISTORY

33 Questions by Thomas E. Woods, Jr
A Century of War by John Denson
A Distant Mirror by Barbara Tuchman
A History of Money and Banking by Murray N. Rothbard

A Nation of Sheep by Andrew Napolitano

Age of Inflation by Hans F. Sennholz

American Empire Before the Fall by Bruce Fein

America's Great Depression by Murray Rothbard

As We Go Marching by John T. Flynn

Basic American Government by Clarence B. Carson

Between The Lines by Walter Beller

Blowback by Chalmers Johnson

Charlie Wilson's War by George Crile

Christianity and War by Laurence M. Vance

Churchill, Hitler, and "The Unnecessary War" by Patrick J. Buchanan

Confessions of an Economic Hit Man by John Perkins

Crisis and Leviathan by Robert Higgs

Death by Government by R. J. Rummel

Democracy: The God That Failed by Hans-Hermann Hoppe

Dice Have No Memory by Bill Bonner

Discovery of Freedom by Rose Wilder Lane

Dred Scott's Revenge by Andrew Napolitano

Emancipating Slaves, Enslaving Free Men by Jeffrey Rogers Hummel

FDR'S Folly by Jim Powell

For Good and Evil by Charles Adams

Forced Into Glory by Lerone Bennett, Jr.

Great Wars and Great Leaders: A Libertarian Rebuttal by Ralph Raico

Hamilton's Curse by Thomas DiLorenzo

How Capitalism Saved America by Thomas DiLorenzo

Inside American Education by Thomas Sowell

King Leopold's Ghost by Adam Hochschild

Lies the Government Told You by Andrew Napolitano

Lincoln Über Alles: Dictatorship Comes to America by John
 Avery Emison
Lincoln Unmasked by Thomas DiLorenzo
Men of Wealth by John T. Flynn
Mencken The American Iconoclast by Marion Elizabeth
 Rodgers
Novus Ordo Seclorum by Forrest McDonald
Pearl Harbor: The Seeds and Fruits of Infamy by Percy L.
 Greaves, Jr.
Reassessing the Presidency by John V. Denson
Roots of American Order by Russell Kirk
The Ascent of Money: A Financial History of the World by Niall
 Ferguson
The Costs of War: America's Pyrrhic Victories by John V. Denson
The Guns of August by Barbara W. Tuchman
The Lysander Spooner Reader with Introduction by George H.
 Smith
The Shadow Factory by James Bamford
Understanding the Modern Culture Wars by Paul A. Cleveland

Books for those who are interested in the Stock Market

*Conquer the Crash: You Can Survive and Prosper in a
 Deflationary Depression* by Robert R. Prechter Jr.
Den of Thieves by James B. Stewart
Devil Take The Hindmost: A History of Financial Speculation by
 Edward Chancellor
Eat the Rich by P.J. O'Rourke
Empire of Debt: The Rise of an Epic Financial Crisis by Bill
 Bonner & Addison Wiggin

Extraordinary Popular Delusions and The Madness of Crowds
by Charles Mackay

FIASCO: The Inside Story of a Wall Street Trader by Frank
Partnoy

*Financial Reckoning Day: Surviving the Soft Depression of the
21st Century* by Bill Bonner & Addison Wiggin

Financial Reckoning Day Fallout by Bill Bonner and Addison
Wiggin

Gents with No Cents by Ron DeLegge

*Inventing Money: The Story of Long-Term Capital Management
and the Legends Behind It* by Nicholas Dunbar

Money & Wealth in the New Millennium by Norm Franz

*Myths, Lies and Downright Stupidity: Get Out the Shovel—
Why Everything You Know if Wrong* by John Stossel

The Battle for the Soul of Capitalism by John C. Bogle

The Creature from Jekyll Island by G. Edward Griffin

The Great Wall Street Retirement Scam by Rick Bueter

The Losing Game: Why You Can't Beat Wall Street by T. E.
Scott

The Pirates of Manhattan by Barry J. Dyke

The Pirates of Manhattan II: Highway to Serfdom by Barry J.
Dyke

The Trouble with Mutual Funds by Richard Rutner

Unmasking the Sacred Lies by Paul Cleveland

*What Goes Up: The Uncensored History of Modern Wall Street
as Told by the Bankers, Brokers, CEOs, and Scoundrels Who
Made It Happen* by Eric J. Weiner

ECONOMICS

The Bible

Against Intellectual Monopoly by Michele Boldrin and David
    K. Levine
Against The Gods: The Remarkable Story of Risk by Peter L.
    Bernstein
Age of Inflation by Hans F. Sennholz
*At the Crest of the Tidal Wave: A Forecast for the Great Bear
    Market* by Robert R. Prechter Jr.
Atlas Shrugged by Ayn Rand
*Back to the Land: Arthurdale, FDR's New Deal, and the Costs of
    Economic Planning* by C. J. Maloney
Basic Economics, Third Edition by Clarence B. Carson and
    Paul A. Cleveland
Becoming Your Own Banker: The Infinite Banking Concept by
    R. Nelson Nash
Boundaries of Order: Private Property as a Social System by
    Butler Shaffer
*Broke: What Every American Business Must Do to Restore
    Our Financial Stability and Protect Our Future* by John
    Mumford
Discovery of Freedom: Man's Struggle Against Authority by
    Rose Wilder Lane
Economics for Real People by Gene Callahan
Economics in One Lesson by Henry Hazlitt
Fiat Money Inflation in France by Andrew Dickson White
For A New Liberty: The Libertarian Manifesto by Murray N.
    Rothbard
Frederic Bastiat: Ideas and Influence by Dean Russell
Going Broke by Degree: Why College Costs Too Much by
    Richard Vedder
High Financier: The Lives and Time of Siegmund Warburg by
    Niall Ferguson

How an Economy Grows and Why It Crashes by Peter D. Schiff

Human Action: A Treatise on Economics by Ludwig von Mises

I.O.U.S.A.: One Nation. Under Stress. In Debt. by Addison
    Wiggin and Kate Incontrera

*Meltdown: A Free-Market Look at Why the Stock Market
    Collapsed, the Economy Tanked, and Government Bailout
    Will Make Things Worse* by Thomas E. Woods Jr.

*Mobs, Messiahs, and Markets: Surviving the Public Spectacle in
    Finance and Politics* by William Bonner and Lila Rajiva

Money, Bank Credit, and Economic Cycles by Jesus Huerta de
    Soto

Nullification: How to Resist Federal Tyranny in the 21st Century
    by Thomas E. Woods Jr.

Our Enemy, the State by Albert J. Nock

Paper Money by Adam Smith

Social Security: False Consciousness and Crisis by John Attarian

Sound and Fury: The Science and Politics of Global Warming by
    Patrick J. Michaels

The Case Against the Fed by Murray Rothbard

The Failure of the New Economics by Henry Hazlitt

The God of the Machine by Isabel Paterson

The Income Tax: Root of all Evil by Frank Chodorov

The Law by Frederic Bastiat

The Mainspring of Human Progress by Henry Grady Weaver

The Man Versus the State by Herbert Spencer

The Mystery of Banking by Murray N. Rothbard

*The Mystery of Capital: Why Capitalism Triumphs in the West
    and Fails Everywhere Else* by Hernando De Soto

The Pension Idea by Paul Poirot

The Road to Serfdom by F. A. Hayek

The Retirement Myth: What You Must Know Now to Prosper in

the Coming Meltdown of Job Security, Pension Plans, Social
Security, the Stock Market, Housing Prices, and More* by
Craig S. Karpel
The Social Security Fraud by Abraham Ellis
Unmasking the Sacred Lies by Paul A. Cleveland

PERSONAL DEVELOPMENT

The Bible
*Start With Why: How Great Leaders Inspire Everyone to Take
Action* by Simon Sinek
The Bait of Satan by John Bevere
The Prayer of Jabez: Breaking Through to the Blessed Life by
Bruce Wilkerson
The Richest Man in Babylon by George S. Clason
The Slight Edge: Secret to a Successful Life by Jeff Olson
*The Sovereign Individual: Mastering the Transition to the
Information Age* by James Davidson, and William Rees-
Mogg
The Strangest Secret by Earl Nightingale
The Twelve Year Sentence edited by William F. Rickenbacker
Think and Grow Rich by Napoleon Hill

RECOMMENDED WEBSITES

The Foundation for Economic Education – www.fee.org
The Ludwig von Mises Institute – www.mises.org
Lew Rockwell – www.lewrockwell.com
Bill Bonner – www.dailyreckoning.com
Lara Murphy Report – http://consultingbyrpm.com

BIOGRAPHY OF R. NELSON NASH

Born in Greensboro, GA in 1931. The third child in a family of four boys.

Married in Athens, GA to Mary Edwards Williams on August 16, 1952.

They have three children, ten grandchildren and three great-grandchildren.

BS Degree in Forestry from University of Georgia, 1952.

First soloed an airplane on October 14, 1946 in Athens, GA. Spent 30 years with the Army National Guard, where he earned Master Aviator Wings.

Consulting Forester for 9 years in eastern North Carolina, 1954–1963.

Life insurance agent with Equitable of New York for 23 years (Hall of Fame member), and The Guardian Life for 12 years.

Chartered Life Underwriter, and Life Member of MDRT. Member of Equitable Life's Hall of Fame.

Discoverer and developer of *The Infinite Banking Concept.* Author of *Becoming Your Own Banker.* Over 200,000 copies sold.

Publisher of BANK NOTES, a quarterly newsletter.

Teacher and lecturer of the banking concept through dividend-paying whole life insurance. He lectures all over the United States, teaching his book in ten hour seminars. He currently averages 50 seminars per year.

He is a passionate student of Austrian Economics, having started this pursuit over 55 years ago.